HEAVEN AND HELL
A message of hope and warning to believers

HEAVEN AND HELL
A message of hope
and warning to believers

David Pawson

Anchor Recordings

First published in Great Britain in 2021 by
Anchor which is a trading name of David Pawson Publishing Ltd
Synegis House, 21 Crockhamwell Road,
Woodley, Reading RG5 3LE

**For more of David Pawson's teaching,
including DVDs and CDs, go to
www.davidpawson.com**

**FOR FREE DOWNLOADS
www.davidpawson.org**

**For further information, email
info@davidpawsonministry.com**

ISBN 978-1-913472-25-2

Printed by Ingram Spark

Contents

This book is based on a series of talks. Originating as it does from the spoken word, its style will be found by many readers to be somewhat different from my usual written style. It is hoped that this will not detract from the substance of the biblical teaching found here.

As always, I ask the reader to compare everything I say or write with what is written in the Bible and, if at any point a conflict is found, always to rely upon the clear teaching of scripture.

David Pawson 1930 - 2020

Chapter 1

THE RETURN OF CHRIST (Part 1)

Many of us have an ambiguous attitude towards the future. We have a mixture of fascination and fear. We would like to know what is going to happen, but then we are not quite sure that we would like to know. Supposing I had a unique gift of knowledge – the word of knowledge – and could actually tell you the date of your death. Would you like to know? Even if it was fifty years in the future would you like to know? No—some, like me, would not believe it if it were fifty years ahead. But, you see, we have got this strange curiosity: we want to know what is going to happen and then we are afraid to know. We don't want to celebrate our death day as well as our birthday every year.

Would you like that, or would you prefer to remain in ignorance? Would you like to know when the world is going to end? Actually, scientists are now telling us a date when they believe the world as we know it will come to an end. But they could be wrong. So, we have this strange ambiguity about the future. There are three ways in which people try to find out about the future. The first one that I want to mention is what I call superstitious divination, clairvoyance, horoscopes. It has been claimed that six out of ten men and seven out of ten women read their horoscope every day in this country. That is why magazines and newspapers have their stars columns. I am happy to tell you that I don't know which sign of the zodiac I was born under and I am not going to tell you my birthday because I don't want you to know.

I would rather remain in ignorance but people try to find out from the stars or from clairvoyants what their future is. Clairvoyants have never been more than five per cent right in their predictions, or, to put it another way, they have all been at least ninety-five per cent wrong. So why do people go to them and why do people read their stars?

The second way of finding out about the future is a little more accurate. I call it the way of scientific deduction. There are now professors of futurology in many universities and what they do is they extrapolate from the present trends into the future and try to work out and guess as reasonably accurately as they can what is going to happen.

The Massachusetts Institute of Technology in America is one of the foremost bodies that is doing this work. Some researchers there have come up with a date for the end of the world, and the date is 2050. They say that given the present population growth and the energy resources and the food resources of our planet, that is the crossover point beyond which life will be impossible unless we can change some of the present trends – unless we can limit population growth or find new sources of energy. So, if it is 2050 then we have got less than thirty years left according to them. Incidentally, scholars in Guildford came up with the same figure. So, 2050 is a figure that is freely being talked about. Scientific deduction about the future is about twenty-five per cent accurate or, to put it negatively, it is about seventy-five per cent wrong.

There is a third way of finding out the future that is even more accurate and that is the way of scriptural declaration.

So, you can go to superstition or you can go to science

or you can go to scripture. Yet few people realise that the Bible is packed with predictions. About one verse in every four in the Bible contains a prediction. Altogether, there are some seven hundred and thirty-five different events that are foretold within the pages of your Bible. How accurate has the Bible been so far? Well, it may be news to you, but five hundred and ninety-six of those predictions have already come true to the letter. That is just over eighty per cent.

That does not mean that only eighty per cent of the Bible's predictions are accurate, because most of the rest are concerned with the end of the world so they could not possibly have happened yet. In fact, there are fewer than twenty yet to happen before the return of Jesus to planet Earth. So far, the Bible has proven to be one hundred per cent accurate in its predictions. So, why do people go to superstition or to science when they could read about the future here, and know that a book that has been right in eighty per cent of its predictions is probably going to be right for the other twenty per cent, especially about the events at the very end of history, the end of our world.

Of all those events out of the seven hundred and thirty-five predictions, there is one that occurs three hundred and eighteen times in the Bible. It is the most frequently mentioned prediction of all, that Jesus Christ, who lived on Earth two thousand years ago, is coming back to Planet Earth. So we are talking about the most predicted event even in the Bible and we are talking about something that is absolutely certain to happen. There are many things we could say about this. But we are going to ask a number of simple questions. First of all, *where* is he coming back to? Secondly, *how* is he coming back? Thirdly, *when* is he coming back? Fourthly, and very much more importantly, *why* is he coming back?

There are plenty of Christians who believe he is coming

back but who have never thought through why he should need to. Did he not do all that he needed to on the first visit? Why would he come back? Then there is the most practical question of all: *how does that affect us?* Let me ask you a question just to whet your appetite. Supposing Jesus were not coming back here at all. Supposing he is staying where he is in heaven and that we will go to join him there when we die and stay there with him forever, and that a new heaven and a new earth will be created after that; supposing he is not coming back here but we are all going to join him there and stay with him there, will that make any difference to the way we live next Monday morning?

Now think it through. It is a good question to ask yourself. Let us go to that first question. Where is he coming back to? I want to say right at the beginning that when he comes back he is not coming to England, nor to America nor to Russia. He is not coming back to any of the world capitals. He is not coming back to any of the religious capitals. He is not coming to Rome. He is not coming to Geneva or Canterbury, New York or Beijing. So, where is he coming back to? The answer the Bible gives is quite clear. He is coming back to his own city, the city he called the city of the great king, Jerusalem. That is where we will need to be if we are going to meet him. That is the city he left from and that is the city he is coming back to.

Now, some people vaguely think he is coming back everywhere. I am not quite sure that they have thought out how he can do that, especially since he is coming back in a body and a body locates us in one place and you cannot be in two places at once when you are in a body. So, Jesus is coming back with his body. One tradition says that that body was five feet ten inches tall. I don't know if that is accurate but I mention it just so that you realise that the physical element of this is real. He is coming back in his Jewish body. Therefore, he has got to come back to one place and he cannot come back everywhere at once, which means that we will have to go and join him, and in fact we will. As I shall mention later, you are going to get your first free flight to the Holy Land but he is coming back to a specific place in his body and we shall meet him in that place and that place is Jerusalem. That is the place where everything happened that has enabled us to become Christians.

Let us turn to the second question: how is he coming back? Here I want to draw first of all a tremendous contrast with his first coming. When he came the first time hardly anybody knew. In fact, for the first nine months he was on Earth only two people knew. When he was actually born only a handful of shepherds and a few clever men from the East knew about it. In fact, the whole thing passed almost unnoticed. His first coming would never have got into the press. Nobody took any notice. In fact, the sign in the sky of his first coming was again hardly noticed except by those who were looking hard and studying such things. It was a tiny pinpoint of light that pointed to where he was born, but most people never even noticed that star. In fact, some people have tried to persuade me that the wise men following the star means that astrology is in the Bible and approved. I want to tell you nothing could be further from the truth. The basic belief of astrology is that the position of the stars affects a baby when it is born. But at Bethlehem it was the position of the baby that was affecting the stars and that is completely the opposite. But it was just a tiny pinprick of light that signalled his first coming. We are told that for his Second Coming the entire sky will be lit up like lightning from East to West, and the whole sky will blaze and everybody will know that something of unique significance has happened. So, whereas the first coming was so quiet, so unnoticed, so humble, the Second Coming will be in total contrast to that. In fact, I want to give you a little

Greek lesson. There are three Greek words that are used in the New Testament about his Second Coming which were not used about the first, each of which is very significant.

The first is the word *parousia*, which means an important arrival. It was used in the ancient world of the arrival of a royal personage – the king or queen coming to visit. It was also used of an invading army. For instance, when D-Day arrived it was a *parousia* because something was going to happen that would change the whole situation. So that is the first word. It is an arrival of tremendous significance.

The second Greek word I want to pass on to you is *epiphania*, which means not to arrive but to appear. Have you ever been in Pall Mall, standing around the Victoria monument on a national occasion, and looked up at the balcony of Buckingham Palace, that first-floor balcony, and waited for those French doors to be opened by the footmen, and then the Royal Family appears on the balcony – the moment that everybody has been awaiting? A great cry goes up from the crowd, from excitement. That is what this second word means. It means to come out onto the balcony where everybody can see you and to appear before the people. Jesus did not do that on his first coming.

The third word is *apokalupsis* and that word means to be uncovered – not to appear naked but to appear as you really are. Therefore, you will not see a baby lying in a manger on his Second Coming. He will appear, as he really is, the Son of God in all his glory. If you have ever seen the Queen arriving for the opening of Parliament you will have noticed how she has her crown and jewels and sits in all her glory. She appears as the Queen of England, and when Jesus comes back he will appear as he is. He will be uncovered and people will see his glory. When he came the first time that glory was covered up, and all the paintings depicting him with a halo are quite inaccurate. He did not walk around with a halo.

In fact, if he did, people would have asked questions but, in fact, they saw no beauty that they should desire him. To most people he was simply a carpenter from Nazareth. That glory was hidden, but when he comes a second time it will not be hidden at all. Everybody will see. Therefore, there is a very great contrast between his first coming and his Second Coming. But there is not a contrast between his first going and his Second Coming. Does that sound a bit odd to you? Let me explain what I mean. Supposing you had been on the Mount of Olives with a video camera on the day that Jesus ascended into heaven and went back home to be with his Father. Supposing you had been able to take a video of him ascending until he disappeared up into the clouds, supposing that you had that video, and supposing you could then play it backwards, you would have an exact film of his Second Coming because the angels at his Ascension said to the men who were gazing up into heaven, "Why do you go on gazing up into heaven? He will come back in exactly the same way as you saw him go." So whereas his Second Coming is a complete contrast to his first coming, it is exactly the same as his first going, except that it will be in reverse and he will appear out of the clouds. By the way, that means that it will be a west wind at the time. I am able to say that because in Israel they only get clouds if the wind is from the west. When it comes from any other direction it comes from the desert and it is a dry, hot wind, but when it comes from the Mediterranean it picks up moisture and you can see a little cloud forming that is no bigger than a man's hand, that will get bigger and bigger and then you will have rain. So, we know the wind will be from the west. Once again, in mentioning this I want you to realise that we are talking about reality and not something in a stained glass window or a fairy tale. We are talking about something that will actually happen in this world of ours with the wind blowing from the west and those cumulus clouds. I love flying above clouds, don't you? Looking down on the sunlit clouds from above is the nearest thing you will see, in physical terms, to the *shekinah* glory of God. Because always you find clouds associated with the glory of the Lord and I am sure that cumulus clouds are the nearest to that glory, the way they mount up like a mountain range with the sun shining on them.

So that is how he will come. I have told you what you can see but I had better tell you what you will hear. If you don't like noisy meetings then you had better not be around on that occasion. It will be the noisiest meeting that has ever been held, as well as the biggest. My grandfather, who was a pastor, is buried in Newcastle upon Tyne and on his gravestone are three words. They are not Rest in Peace, and they are not from the Bible. They are from the hymnbook. They are from an old Methodist hymn and these are the three words: "What a meeting!" I think people must stand and look at that gravestone and wonder what on earth this means.

Christians sometimes get their diaries filled up with meetings, but what a meeting that will be! It will be the biggest, and there won't be a stadium on earth to hold it so we are going to have to hold it in the air. That will be when you get your free flight to the Holy Land. But the noise! There will be archangels shouting their heads off, there will be trumpets blowing enough noise to raise the dead, and, in fact, that will happen. Here is a lovely thought: don't worry about dying before this happens because if you die before it happens you will get a front seat. That is what my Bible says. Paul says to the Thessalonians, "Don't grieve about those who have already died. They are not going to miss anything." Far from it! When he descends from heaven with the sound of a trumpet, the dead will rise first, so that means they will get there first and we who are alive will catch up with them.

So, Paul says, "Encourage each other with these words."

If you die first you will get a front seat, so we win either way. If we don't die first, we will get a new body straight away and no undertaker's measurements will be required, so it is good news. That is how he is going to appear. There will be millions upon millions. There are now 2.4 billion people who profess to believe in Jesus, so that really will be a big meeting. To say nothing of all the angels, and there are myriads of them and they will be joining in too. I can't imagine what the singing is going to be like. Now when will he come? Here we run into problems. Christians are very good at trying to guess dates. I just jotted down a few of the dates that leading Christians have mentioned. There was a man called Miller and he said it would be 1843. By the way, if you are going to guess the date of the Second Coming my advice is to guess a date well after you will be here because then you won't have to be around to face the music. It is much wiser to think of one well ahead rather than one in the immediate future but Miller said it was 1843 and that prediction came from the Seventh-day Adventist movement.

Then there was a man called Russell and he said it would be 1914, and from him came the Jehovah's Witness movement, but lest you think that it is only cults or sects that guess the date of the Second Coming, let me tell you that Martin Luther said it would be 1636. Now that was "wise" because he said he would be dead by then. John Wesley was equally "wise" when he said 1874 and most Christians love to try to work it out and get the little programmes, and get the details together. In our day, there have been a lot of people saying, "We are the last generation." Have you heard that one? A lot of people have asked me, "Do you think it will be in our lifetime?" Every generation hopes for this.

But Jesus himself said, "Of that day or of that hour knows no one, not even the Son. The Father only keeps that date." So, it is a good thing to be very cautious when somebody tells you, "I know the date." Having said that, I am going to tell you that I think I know the month, although I don't know the year. I shall return to that shortly. Now, if Jesus himself was unaware of the date are we likely to know it? Nevertheless, his disciples did ask him: "Jesus, what will be the signs of your coming, the signals of your coming? How will we know when it is going to happen?" Jesus actually gave them signals. He gave them signs. He said, "You are to watch and pray." What are we to watch for? You can't watch for his coming, otherwise you would have to walk around all day looking at the sky. He didn't mean watch for his coming. He said, "Watch for the signs of my coming." He told us exactly what they are. Now, many years ago I used to go and look at trains. I still do, actually. But as a boy I used to love to be a trainspotter, and, in those days, it was the London and Northeast Railway (LNER) that ran through my home town of Newcastle upon Tyne. What you may not know is that just outside Newcastle Central Station was the biggest railway crossing in the whole world. I used to go and stand at the end of the platform there, overlooking that huge crossing where all the lines from London and the South crossed with all the lines from Scotland and the North. It is by far the best place to go trainspotting in the entire country. We learned early on to watch for the signals that would tell us when the train was coming.

There were four signals you watched for. In those days, the signals were not electric light bulbs. They were a big arm that went down and up again. Do you remember those? There was the distance signal, which was a yellow one with black stripes on it with a kind of fork at the end. That was the distance signal that was the furthest out. Then there was the outer home signal, a red one. Then the inner home and finally there was what was called the starter signal, which was right at the platform and actually cleared the train to start from the platform, so it was saying: the next bit of line is open. We used to watch these four signals. When the distant one went down you knew the train was a few miles away. The outer home signal went down when the train was in the next section.

With the inner home signal you got really excited because you knew the train was around the bend, and by the time the starter went down, there it was. You could tell how near the train was. Now Jesus gave his followers four signals, four signs, and they are very clear. He said that these were the signals to watch for. He said: The first you will see in the world out there, so watch the world for the first signal. The second will be in the church, so watch the church for the second signal. The third will be in the Middle East, so watch the Middle East for the third signal. The fourth will be in the sky and you will see that signal in the sky.

Christians get into such a muddle about all these signs but I have taken these four signs straight from Jesus. My principle is to start with what Jesus said and fit everything else in the Bible into what he said. He gave us this very simple framework into which you can fit all the other details. The first signal is in the world and consists of disasters. Jesus mentioned three in particular: earthquakes, wars and famines. He said: "You are going to see more and more of those."

I was in the Philippines in the city of Baguio. I had not heard that they had had such a bad earthquake but I stood and looked at the appalling ruin of the Hyatt International Hotel. Fifteen storeys, and it had just collapsed. They were spraying disinfectant with a hosepipe on the ruins because they could not get any of the bodies out. All the American and Japanese tourists were buried under it; streets opened up in great cracks. I had never actually been in an earthquake like that so I could not imagine what it must have been like.

Famines: there are plenty of those around, and increasing. Wars: I had not realised there have been two hundred conflicts since World War Two, some of which are ongoing. Jesus said that when you hear all these things, that is sign number one.

He said, "Don't let your hearts be troubled" because that is not the end but the beginning. These are not death pangs but birth pangs. It is painful but it is the pain of contractions of a new universe coming. Now that puts a whole different light on it. It does not mean that Christians are callous or unsympathetic toward the victims of these disasters but we don't say, "I don't know what things are coming to." We say, "I do know what things are coming to." There is a good line for you when you want to witness. When anybody says, "I don't know what the world is coming to," quietly say, "I do," and see what happens. You will get a good opening. But Jesus teaches that these are like the first contractions an expectant mother feels. They are the beginning of something, not the end of something.

Something is going to be born out of all this pain, this travail. Something is going to be born of the universe labouring. Paul actually talks about the whole creation groaning and travailing. You can hear earthquakes. They groan. They travail. So, earthquakes are natural disasters. Wars are human-caused disasters. Famines can be a bit of both. But Jesus says that is the beginning of the end. But it is a beginning that follows, so don't let your hearts be troubled. He warns you that when all these disasters are filling the world, that will give a unique opportunity for false messiahs, false christs to arise. We are getting a whole lot of them. I once read in a weekend magazine of a man who said, "I am Yahweh and I have come to save the world." These individuals have been popping up all over the place.

You see, when the world is shaking with disaster after

disaster, people look for someone to help them out of their trouble. They look for somebody they can trust and look to a strong man. That gives a unique opportunity for false christs. We can expect a growing number of such false messiahs to appear in our day because of all the disasters that are coming. So we have now seen sign number one, and the danger that accompanies sign number one: the danger of false christs, but it is highly unlikely that Christians will be fooled by false christs.

I had a letter from someone some time ago from Staffordshire, which said, "Dear David, I bought one of your tapes thinking you were a gospel singer but I was disappointed to find that there was no music, only talk. But I have listened to the tape and I am the one you were talking about. I am the Christ. I have come to save the world." He spent fourteen pages telling me this, in good grammar, excellent handwriting. We are going to see an awful lot of this as disasters shake people; it provides a spiritual vacuum into which false messiahs can step.

Now for signal number two. This will be in the church and consists of three features, just as the first signal consists of three features, three kinds of disaster: earthquake, war, and famine. The second signal has three parts to it but this time they all appear in the church. Number one is *universal persecution*, the church hated by all the nations and under pressure everywhere. Now that has never actually happened in the last two thousand years but it is nearer to happening now than it has ever been. Out of some hundred and ninety-three nation states in our world there are fewer than two dozen where the church is not under pressure. The number is getting smaller. In fact, the first signs of pressure on Christians are appearing here in "Christian" England. The pressure is really going to be on us, notably as we are beginning to see at the moment, in the education sphere, but

Equalities legislation is going to be used against Christians.

So, the pressure is going to be on us here. Jesus said the first part of the second signal will be universal pressure on the church. The second part of that sign follows from the first. He said the love of many will grow cold. In other words, pressure sorts out the nominal Christians from the genuine ones. Those who are Sunday Christians or churchgoers will soon disappear under pressure. I heard of a prayer meeting many years ago in one of the countries behind the Iron Curtain and two soldiers with machine guns burst into the prayer meeting and said, "We're going to kill the Christians." The Christians thought they were drunk but they were sober. Then they said, "If you're not a Christian, get out." A number got up and ran.

Then the two soldiers said to the rest, "Now will you please tell us how to become Christians? We had to make sure of you before we talked to you." Well, how would that affect your church prayer meeting? You see, Jesus said there will be universal pressure and the result will be a falling away of nominal Christians. Now that is not bad news. That is good news because the third part of the signal is this: Jesus said that the gospel will be preached to all the nations. In other words, when the pressure is on the church it sorts the church out and refines the church and the church is far better able to get on with the job that Jesus left us to do, namely to evangelise the nations, something that you can see happening. You can see it happening in China today. There are villages in China where eighty-five per cent of the population has been born again. It is the church under pressure and that gets rid of nominal churchgoers who can't do the job anyway. That kind of church under pressure grows very fast.

Don't ever pity churches that are being persecuted. Envy them. I remember going to the former Czechoslovakia years ago and we told them we prayed for them in England. They said, "You pray for us? Why? We hold prayer meetings for the church in England because you are in a far more needy state than we are." That put us in our place and humbled us. So that is the second signal to look for: pressure on the church in every country of the world, nominal Christians falling away, and the rest preaching the gospel to all the nations and getting the job done. That is signal number two.

Signal number three, he said, will be in the Middle East. Here Jesus quoted from the prophet Daniel: an extraordinary term which Daniel uses three times in his predictions about the future, namely "The abomination of desolation". That is an inadequate translation. I am afraid we haven't words bad enough in English really to communicate the horror of that Hebrew expression. It means something disgusting, abhorrent and offensive. In a sense, it came true before Jesus came. It came true when a man called Antiochus Epiphanes, a Greek emperor, strolled into Jerusalem at the head of an army and did the most unspeakable things.

He went into the temple at Jerusalem and he sacrificed a pig on the altar, pork on the altar, then he turned the little vestries (the rooms around the side of the temple) into prostitutes' brothels, and that was what happened. It was the most disgusting, blasphemous act that has ever happened in Jewish history. They have referred to Antiochus Epiphanes as the abomination of desolation. In a sense he was, or rather he was a foretaste of that. But towards the end of history we shall see a man described by Paul in 2 Thessalonians 1 as the man of lawlessness, a man who says, "I acknowledge no law but my own will"; a man who sets himself up as god, and in the very place where God's name has been placed. Watch the Middle East for that man to appear, for that dreadful thing to happen again, a man defying God in the main place where God's name is acknowledged as being holy.

Jesus says, "Those who are living in that area around Jerusalem, as soon as that man appears, get out, go as quickly as you can. Don't stop to pack, just get out and flee quickly." But the message is: the rest of you in the rest of the world, stay put, stay right where you are. Don't move. "Above all," said Jesus, "trust your eyes not your ears. You will hear rumours that I have come here, that I've come there. Don't listen to rumours. Don't let your ears, don't let anything you hear mislead you. You just keep watching for me."

By the way, I should have mentioned that the danger when that second signal appears will be the danger of false prophets. I am afraid that while Christians are not prone to believing false messiahs in the church, they are peculiarly prone to believing false prophets. We know what false prophets say. They always say, "Peace, peace" when there is no peace. They always say, "Don't worry, it won't happen." They always want to calm and comfort people. True prophets tell the truth even if it hurts. So, we have signal number one in the world: disasters and the danger of false messiahs being followed by the world. Signal number two is pressure on the universal church, with nominal Christians falling away and the rest getting the job of preaching the gospel done. The danger will be false prophets who will tell the church not to worry, that it is all right, it is not going to get any worse. In the third signal the danger, said Jesus, will be false messiahs and false prophets. What a crisis that will bring to us! We will really have to be very sure of our faith then. We must not listen.

I am afraid Christians are pretty good gossips, aren't we? Have you heard the latest? Jesus taught: Use your eyes not your ears. Watch. There will be plenty of false prophets telling you what God is saying. There will be plenty of false messiahs telling you that they are the Christ, because wherever there is a dead body the vultures gather, and they are vultures and they are just picking stuff up for themselves out of the mess. Now, at the third signal I want you to notice two things. First, I want you to notice that Christ has not come yet. You may hear that he has come but Christ says: don't pay any attention. Christ has not come. The second thing I want you to notice carefully, and this is quite far-reaching, is that the Christians have not gone yet. I put those two things together. Here we have got this major crisis in the Middle East, this man of lawlessness otherwise known as Antichrist, and all kinds of things. We have this third signal along with the political situation in the Middle East, and isn't that entirely credible now? But Christ has not come yet and Christians have not gone yet.

So, we come to the fourth and last signal. This will be in the sky. This is what the signal will be: the sun will be switched off; the moon will be switched off; the stars will be switched off one by one until the entire sky is totally black and there is no natural light whatsoever. Now this fourth signal gets me excited. I remember as a little boy being taken to a theatre to see a Christmas pantomime. I recall it vividly. It was the Theatre Royal in Newcastle upon Tyne and I remember sitting there in the balcony and looking at the stage. There was a bit of excitement. Everybody was chattering. Lots of families were there for the Christmas panto, and one by one the house lights went out until we were sitting in the dark. I remember now my little heart beating, "It's about to start." Silence fell. Then the stage curtains went to the side and there was a blaze of light and it all happened.

Now that is exactly what the fourth signal will be. God will switch every other light out so that the glory of Jesus will be the only light, like lightning from east to west, from horizon to horizon. There will be just one blaze of light but it won't be from the sun, the moon or the stars. Now I told you what the danger is when the other three signals appear. The danger of the first is false messiahs, the danger of the second is false prophets, the danger of the third is false prophets and messiahs. What will be the danger of the fourth signal? Nothing. It will be over too quickly. So, when you get that signal, hold on to your hat because you will be off. You will hear something. You will hear that trumpet. You will hear a great trumpet blast, so when you see all the lights go out and see this flash of lightning from one horizon to the other and you hear that blast of a trumpet that will echo around the globe, you will hang on because you will be going to meet him.

Now that is the answer to when he is going to come except for one little thing. I mentioned earlier that I thought I knew the month because, you see, Jesus did everything according to God's calendar. On God's calendar there are three great times of the year: Passover, Pentecost and Tabernacles. Jesus died at the Passover and he sent his Spirit at Pentecost but he hasn't yet fulfilled Tabernacles. Mind you, if you study your Bible carefully, you will find that Jesus was born during that Feast of Tabernacles in late September or early October. The Word became flesh and tabernacled among us, said John, but if you work it out, that is when he was born. You know he was not born in December. He was born at the end of September or the beginning of October, but I believe his Second Coming will be right on time, not least because the Feast of Tabernacles is preceded by the Feast of Trumpets and every mention of trumpets in the New Testament is to announce the coming of the Lord Jesus. So one of these years in September or October he will be back but I can't tell you which year. We will now move on to the more important questions: why is he coming back and what difference does that make to the way we live now?

Chapter 2

THE RETURN OF CHRIST (Part 2)

I have given you four signals or signs that Jesus gave us for his return to Planet Earth. Of those four I would say that we have seen one and a half already, but with the speed of world events, who can say how long it will take for the other two and a half to catch up? Indeed, the world is changing so fast that we cannot be dogmatic about it. But a far more important question than "*When* will he come?" is "*Why* will he come?" This is a very real question. There must be some very big reason why he has to return.

One of the surprises in the New Testament is a verse in Hebrews which says that he will appear a second time to bring salvation to those who are waiting for him. Now there is a puzzle. Did he not bring us salvation the first time? And you notice that he is coming the second time not to bring salvation to the world or the unbeliever, but to us who are waiting for him. The answer is, of course, that we are not saved yet. We are *being* saved. Salvation is a process and there is one part of me that is not saved yet — a part that you can see. My body is not saved yet, it is still under the law of sin and death. My body will die and rot, provided he does not come back in the meantime.

So, why should he have to come back to complete our

salvation? Now make no mistake about it, he has done all he needs to do to obtain holiness and forgiveness for us. He has not got to die on a cross again, that is all finished with, that is complete. But there are some things that are not yet complete and he is coming back to bring total salvation to those of us who are waiting for him.

There are five reasons why he is coming back, and any of them by themselves would not be, I think, an adequate reason for coming. The first is very simple: to collect us, to meet with us, and to take us to be with him. He said, "If it were not so, I would have told you. I'm going to prepare a place for you," which means that Jesus has gone back to being a carpenter, getting the place ready for us. Did you realise that? He is very good at making things and he is getting your room ready in his Father's house. Then he says, "I will come again and take you to be with me, that where I am you may be too."

I once spoke to an elderly lady in a group of church members who had gone to Israel, and she was wandering around the Arab souk, that underground maze of little shops that constitutes the old Bazaar. She was trying to find the post office to buy a stamp to send a postcard to her daughter. She said to an Arab shopkeeper, "Where is the post office here?" He said, "Well, go down this alleyway, look for an opening on the left, go up some stairs, go up until you come to a fork, turn right, look out for the second turning on the right down that alleyway." The more he spoke the more bewildered she looked.

He realised that she would never be able to find it so he turned around and he closed his little shop, padlocked the shutters and took her by the elbow. He said, "I am the way." He took her to the post office. She was so excited when she came back to the rest of the group and she said, "Guess what I learned this morning?" She said, "I've always wondered what Jesus meant when he said, 'I am the way.'" She continued: "Now I know. It means he'll take me there. I don't need to know the route, he'll take me there."

That is what Jesus is coming to do. He is coming to collect the Christians, which means that if he is coming back to Planet Earth, so am I. If you belong to Christ, so are you. Has that thought struck you before? That if Jesus is coming back here, so are you. Have you ever told your friends that long after your death you are coming back to Planet Earth? Not as a reincarnation, because when you believe in reincarnation you don't know who you are going to come back as—you might come back as a duck, you just don't know. Christians are coming back to Planet Earth as themselves. We will know who we are—we'll be back here.

Do you realise that it is here that we are going to get our new bodies? Not up in heaven, but back here. We will be raised from the dead and given new bodies here. I can't wait to get my new body. Do you know how old I'll be then? Well, I'm in my old age now and some days I feel it. My children think I have one foot in the grave and the other on a banana skin, but anyway here I am. When I get my new body, I'll be thirty-three because my Bible says I'll get a glorious body just like his, and how old is his? I can't wait to be thirty-three again.

I was speaking at a funeral down in the West Country and a lovely Christian brother had died. He got to a good age, but he died of a horrible disease, which made him quite ugly to look at in the last few months. During the funeral I happened to say, "Next time you see him he'll be thirty-three." His widow and daughter almost went hysterical with joy. Afterwards, I asked them why they had that reaction. The widow said, "Well, I was going through his papers last night and I came across a photograph of him when he was young and handsome with thick dark hair. I said to the photograph,

'That's how I'll remember you, darling, not as you were at the end.'" And she said, "That photograph was taken when he was thirty-three."

The daughter said, "That night I had a dream about my daddy. We were playing at the seaside, splashing each other in the water and I felt so happy, and suddenly I woke up and it was just a dream." But she said, "I realised the dream was actually a memory of a childhood holiday." She continued, "We were at the seaside when I was nine years old and when I was nine daddy was thirty-three." So, no wonder they reacted so joyfully to my news.

You see, we are going to get new bodies. Jesus isn't just in the business of saving our souls. He is interested in bodies too. He is interested in the whole of creation. That whole creation is groaning and travailing, waiting for me to get my new body, because when I get my whole new body that will be the signal for the whole of creation to get its new body. All that is going to happen back here. This is where resurrection takes place. This is where bodies are needed and bodies are recreated.

So that is the first reason why he is coming back, to meet with us and to give us our new bodies—right here on Planet Earth. We are going to meet him right here, even if we have died in the meantime. The second reason why he is coming back, and not just coming back to collect Christians, is to convert Jews. They are still his chosen people. God hates divorce and he has not divorced Israel and one of the most amazing mysteries that is revealed to us in scripture is that God has a future plan for the Jewish people.

What will they feel when they see Jesus of Nazareth? Well, the Bible tells us how they will feel. It says they will mourn as for an only son when they realise the tragedy of all these centuries when they missed their own Messiah. Can you imagine it? All the suffering they have been through, all the needless anguish they have had—they will weep. There is only one thing a Jew needs to become a believer in Jesus, and that is to know that he is alive. That is what happened to Paul on the Damascus road.

I was once preaching near Ely in Cambridgeshire and there was a Jewess in the congregation, an attractive lady of about twenty-five or twenty-six years of age. She came to me afterwards. She said, "Mr Pawson, are you trying to tell me that Jesus of Nazareth is still alive?" I said, "That's what I'm saying." And she said, "Then if he is, he must be our Messiah!" You noticed the little personal possessive pronoun "our". "Yes, he is Jewish, for salvation is of the Jews," I said. "That's right," she said, and continued: "How can I find out if he's alive?" I said, "You can try talking to him right now." And she did.

You know, within ten minutes she was teaching me the Bible—she had got it all except the one vital clue. She said, "Then this, then this, then this!" I envy the Jewish people; they have got it there, except for that vital clue. What will happen when the whole nation sees the one whom they have pierced? Jesus still loves his Jewish people—they are his brethren. He is coming back to Jerusalem, and it must be a Jewish city when he comes back, a city which has some bearing on current affairs.

Third reason: he is coming back to conquer his enemies. The last time he came to Jerusalem he came riding on a donkey, but this time he will come on a horse—that is a big difference. A prince of peace uses a donkey; a man of war uses a horse. It is another contrast between his first visit and his second. He comes to Jerusalem to fight and to deal with his enemies. We are told in the Bible that history will be in the control of three persons at the end, presenting a kind of unholy trinity, a kind of inferior substitute for Father, Son and Holy Spirit. In place of Father there will be the devil; in place of Christ there will be the Antichrist; in place of the Holy Spirit there will be the false prophet. Here we have this unholy trinity controlling the situation and Jesus is going to deal with all three. He is coming to fight them and to conquer them and to deal with them once and for all.

I want to shout Hallelujah! He's going to finish them off— that will finish off evil. So, he is coming back to finish off the devil in particular and he is coming back as a lion rather than a lamb, although that word Lamb is misleading. I don't like to talk about the Lamb of God because that makes me think of a little white cuddly woolly thing a few weeks old, but a lamb in scripture is always one year old with horns. It is a male lamb in its prime. I prefer to talk of Jesus as the Ram of God. He is the Lion of Judah, the Ram of God, both very strong pictures. He is coming back to conquer.

"Sing we the King who is coming to reign.
Glory to Jesus, the Lamb that was slain."

Evil will end, good will triumph, which means that we are living in a moral universe. Now that is a very important insight. Most people say, "this universe is not moral. The wicked get away with things, good people suffer, there's no morality in our universe." They see evil triumph and they see good wiped out. Well, we can say this: "It is going to be moral because Jesus is coming back to deal with all evil."

The question arises, why didn't he deal with evil on his first trip? Why didn't he defeat Satan once and for all on his first trip? Why didn't he banish all antichrists and false prophets on his first trip? The answer is very simple. If Jesus had wiped out all evil on his first visit then who would be left? We always assume we would be. Isn't that strange? "Why doesn't he come and deal with *them*?"—that's our cry. We don't cry, "Why doesn't he come and deal with us? Why doesn't he come to stop me spoiling his world?"

We never talk like that—we always think of others. Isn't that interesting? But if Jesus had wiped out all evil people and things when he came the first time you would not be reading this book right now. I'll tell you something else: you wouldn't be here to read it, because if the Lord dealt with us as we deserve we wouldn't be alive today. It is in his mercy that he came the first time to give us a chance to put things right, before he comes to deal with all the things that are wrong. That is why, though the Jews expected the Messiah to come once, the great secret of the New Testament is that the Messiah is coming twice; the first time to get us forgiveness and holiness, the second time to get rid of all evil. Thank the Lord he didn't do it the other way around or none of us would have had a chance. That is the great secret of the kingdom, that the kingdom is coming in two stages.

The next reason why he is coming back is he is going to judge the world. Now here is an eye-opener. God the Father is not going to judge the human race. He has delegated that responsibility to his Son. It is not before God that we shall stand, but before his Son, Jesus. Now I can think of a very good reason why God has decided this. If mankind stood before God the Father on his throne we could say, "God, you're not the one who's able to judge us, because you don't know what it's like being a human being. You don't know what the pressures are like on Earth. You don't know what it's like to be tempted. You don't understand what it's like to be hated. You don't understand what it's like to be accused of a crime you've never committed—you don't understand." But nobody will be able to talk to the Judge like that, because he does understand.

He knows what it is like to be falsely accused of a crime. He knows what it is like to be born illegitimate. He knows what it is like to be tempted at all points. He is the one who is going to judge. Therefore, we must say that Pontius Pilate will one day be judged by Jesus, and Mohammed will one day be judged by Jesus, and Buddha will one day be judged by Jesus, and Confucius will one day be judged by Jesus, and Gorbachev will be judged by Jesus, Saddam Hussein will be judged by Jesus, David Pawson will be judged by Jesus, but we must all stand before the judgment seat of Christ to receive judgment according to the things done in the body. That is the subject for the next chapter—The Day of Judgment. It is Jesus who judges. It is a very important point. Paul, preaching on Mars Hill in Athens, said that God has appointed a day whereby he will judge the world by a man. It is a human being who will judge the ungodly.

I still don't think we have hit the biggest reason why he has to come back here to do this. Why couldn't all this happen elsewhere? Why couldn't it happen in the world of disembodied spirits in Hades? Why does it have to happen here? Why does he have to come back to Planet Earth? There is a fifth reason, though I am going to be frank and say that not all Christians agree with me on this fifth reason. However, there is not the space here to give you all my reasons for believing it.

Nevertheless, I will just state that I believe he is coming back to rule the world—to reign here for a limited time. This is the most incredible part of the story. Human reason or imagination would have guessed it, but there at the end of the Bible we are told that when he has come back, conquered his enemies, cleaned this world up, then he is going to reign right here, and show this world what it can be like when he is in charge.

The world has seen what it is like when Satan is controlling it. The prince of this world has had his day and I believe that God in his amazing wisdom is going to let this world see what it can be like when Jesus is running it. It is called the Millennium, which is a Latin word meaning a thousand years, and that is the figure given for this reign on earth. I have looked everywhere I can at this and found so many different views. There are people who say they are premillennial, postmillennial, amillennial. Have you heard all this? A friend of mine said, "That is a pre-post-erous question!" Nevertheless, I have to tell you that I believe it is plainly taught in scripture that Jesus will reign here before the end of the world and that he will take over the thrones of the nations. Then you will see come true the prophecy that nations will learn multilateral disarmament, "beat their swords into ploughshares, and their spears into pruning hooks". Of course, he will need a government to help him and that is where the Bible, I believe, promises we shall reign with him, which gives a very good reason for us coming back here too, and getting new bodies at the same time.

The whole thing almost defies imagination. For almost three hundred years the early church universally believed this and then I am afraid it came to this new idea that the church would build this new Millennium before Jesus got back—a man called Augustine set that one off. Of course, in those days it looked as if the church was going to win: the Emperor himself had been converted, persecution stopped, and it looked as if the Church was going to take over the world. Well, I'm afraid it no longer looks like that.

Jesus never taught us to believe it would. Jesus taught us that the wheat and the tares would grow together. The kingdom of God is going to get stronger, the kingdom of Satan is going to get stronger, until Christ comes to deal with it and clears the place up. But I do believe that before the final events Jesus will reign over the nations. They will see that he is already King of England. Australia will see it, America, Russia.

Can you imagine the peace and prosperity that will come when Jesus is running this world? After all, God made this world as a present for his Son Jesus. I can't believe that the God who vindicates righteousness would not vindicate his own Son in the eyes of the world. To me that is the biggest reason and the one that justifies his whole return. Without that I find it difficult to understand why it should all have to happen back here, but if that is the main reason for his coming, that he is coming to restore the kingdom to Israel, and to take over the nations of the world, and to fulfil all the promises that God has made for this world, then it makes total sense to me. But I ask you to study the scripture. You will hear lots of ideas, but that is mine. I ask you to come to your own convictions.

It was Hitler's dream to have a kingdom for a thousand years; the Third Reich was to last a thousand years but it lasted a mere twelve. I believe the reign of Jesus will actually last a thousand years. That is my hope and I look forward to that, don't you? Isn't it wonderful that he will take over the nations? No more elections—a king instead. You see, we are not made for democracy, we are made for a king, but, of course, we can't find the right king, that is our problem. Our gospel is that we have already found the King, the right King, the perfect King to rule the nations.

Let me come finally to the practical side. What difference does all this make to the way we live—from Monday to Friday or right through the week? What difference does it actually make? Hope is a vital dimension of human living. We can't live without it. Hope springs eternally in the human breast. We have to have something in the future to look forward to. All through the ages, men have looked forward to a golden age coming, a utopian age, a new age coming, and it has taken many different forms. Christians believe in the new age, the new age of Jesus, not the one of a syncretistic religion.

It is hope that helps you to cope with the present. It is your hope for what may be ahead that enables you to live with the pressures and the disappointments for today. A person without hope wants to end their life. Hope is absolutely essential and faith and love need hope to keep going, and it is our hope in the future that provides us with this incentive. You see, sinners tend to live in the past, they live in their past habits—they can't break them. Sinners are notorious for nostalgia, but nostalgia isn't what it used to be and we are looking forward to something—much better to look forward than to look back. You get tired of people talking about the good old days, don't you? "When I was a child . . . ." I've got to that age myself, but I'm looking forward, you see.

For the Christian, the best is yet to be and that hope has a profound effect. Let me try to illustrate it. Suppose you moved into a house just outside Ashford in Kent, and you learned that a new motorway was going to be built from the Channel right through your house. Your house was going to be demolished in two years' time, and although you would be compensated, you had just bought it. Now, would you then spend days and days rebuilding the kitchen and refitting the bathroom? Would you make that your perfect, ideal home when you knew it was going to be demolished two years later? Of course you wouldn't.

In the same way, the New Testament says, "Seeing all these things are thus to be dissolved, what manner of people ought you to be?" In other words, we don't belong here, we are just passing through, and a hope of a new heaven and a new earth and a mansion up there changes our ideas about life here—you don't get so locked up in your house here because you are not here for ever, you are only here for a short time.

At the age of eighty, Abraham left a two-storey brick house with central heating and running water in the bedrooms. I know this because archeologists found this was the standard of living in Ur of the Chaldees, in modern-day

Iraq and Abraham left that place and went to live in a tent for the rest of his life at that advanced age. "He was quite happy because he was looking for a city whose builder and maker was God"—and that made all the difference, so that life here didn't matter so much.

On the other hand, supposing the British Museum got in touch with you and asked you if you had any crafts or hobbies and you said that you did woodwork, tapestry or needlework. And the British Museum said, "We want a typical example of British amateur craftsmanship for the future and we're going to put it in the Museum forever so that people will always be able to see the kind of thing we did." Now, how much care would you take over that? That would be the best thing you ever made, wouldn't it? Knowing that it was going to be on show for as long as the world was here—you would really do that carefully.

Do you see how your thinking about the future has changed you? If your house is going to be demolished that changes your attitude towards the house, and you don't care so much about a leaking drain or something. Why bother if it is going to be pulled out anyway? But on the other hand, if you know you are doing something that is going to last for a very long time and be seen by a lot of people you will take far more care over it. I am trying to get you to realise that it is how we think about the future that affects how we behave in the present.

There are four things that profoundly affect a believer's life when they realise that Jesus is coming back to Planet Earth—four things, and here they are. I should just add that I was expounding Matthew chapter twenty-four when I gave you the four signs, and I am now going to talk about Matthew 25, which follows it. Having given the signs, Jesus then said, "This is how you are to be ready." He told four parables or four stories. One was about the ten virgins, one was about the talents, one was about sheep and goats, to tell us how to be ready, and what a difference it makes to realise that the Master is coming back one day.

Here are the four things that will be characteristic of Christians who are constantly thinking about the return of the Lord. First, faithful service. Faithful service, because, you see, when he comes back, he will not so much be interested in what you are doing at that time as what you were doing while he was away. Now this is so important because some people panic and think, "My, the Lord may be coming next Tuesday, I must. . ." and they change their patterns of behaviour radically because they don't want to be found doing what they are doing now. But Jesus will not come back and say, "What are you doing at this moment of my return?" He will come back and say, "What were you doing all the time I was away?"

In each of those parables in Matthew 25 there is the phrase "a long time coming," "the bridegroom was a long time coming." The real test of whether you are ready for his return is not what you do if you think he is coming soon, but what you do if you think he is not coming soon. Do you follow me in that? It is a very important point, because what he wants to find is faithful servants. He wants to be able to say, "Well done, even though I was a long time coming you kept at it. You were faithful." So there is this panic, "He might come tonight," or "he might come this week." It does not usually last when he doesn't come tonight or this week, it tends to die off. The motivation is not for when he comes, but for what he will say when he comes. What he wants to be able to say is, "Well done good and faithful servant."

D. L. Moody, the great evangelist of a bygone era, said this: "Ever since I heard that Jesus is coming back to Planet Earth I have wanted to work three times as hard." Faithful service is the first thing that will happen. When I say faithful service, I am not talking about church work. Please understand me, the idea is around that it is only missionaries and pastors that are really in the service of the Lord. That is fostered by the fact that we stick a missionary's photographs up in the porch and we make so much of this that people have got this order of priorities: missionaries are the best servants of God, pastors second best, evangelists, doctors and nurses come a good third and fourth, maybe teachers fifth, taxi drivers fifty-fifth—you know? Computer operators, way down there. Nothing could be further from the truth.

Look, missionaries and pastors will be made redundant in heaven. Have you ever thought of that? We will have to retrain; we will have to be rehabilitated. Note that when I say faithful service I am talking about your daily work, because there will be jobs for us in the future, and those jobs are directly related to how we do our jobs here. The Lord is more interested in how you work than what your job is. Did you know that? Billy Graham's wife put above the kitchen sink, "Notice: Divine service is held here three times every day." She understood.

Whatever your job, faithful service is doing that job well. There was a surgeon in Beijing in China. She was the chief surgeon in a hospital there. She became a Christian and she was sacked. The result was that she was then given the job of cleaning out the toilets, but she said, "I'll clean out the toilets as if Jesus is going to sit on them." She was in full-time Christian work. Never say, "I'm in a secular job." Nothing is secular except sin—faithful service.

Number two: global evangelism. You see, Jesus left us a job to do and it has not been completed. He said, "The gospel must be preached to all nations, then shall the end come. Go and make disciples of all ethnic groups, go and preach the gospel to every creature." We are a long way off that; we are getting nearer to it, but there is an unfinished task of evangelising the world. The more you think about the Lord's return the more you will want to be involved in some way in global evangelism.

Thirdly, there is social reform. Now this may come as a surprise to you, but those who think most about the return of the Lord and the new world that is coming are actually those who want to make this world better. That may sound as if it doesn't work, but in fact it does. If you go to Piccadilly Circus, you will see an aluminium statue of an angel in the middle. It is called "Eros"—that is a terrible name for it. It should be called "Agape", because it is a memorial to Anthony Ashley-Cooper, the Earl of Shaftesbury. Lord Shaftesbury worked all his life to get children out of the factories and to introduce proper working hours and proper living wages. He fought for that on this ground, at the top of every letter he ever wrote to a politician or anyone else, he wrote: "Even so, come Lord Jesus." That was the motivation. He wanted to make this world the best place he could make it because he knew Jesus was coming. Social reform is one of the fruits of a vivid sense of Jesus' return.

Finally, personal holiness. The New Testament says, "Whoever has this hope of him appearing purifies himself, because we know that when he appears we shall be like him, for we shall see him as he is." Or to put it another way, I was speaking in a school to children and a little boy asked, "Why wasn't Jesus married?" I said, "It's all right, he's going to be." The headmaster in his office afterwards said to me, "What was that you said about Jesus getting married?" He said, "I've never heard that before." I said, "The whole Bible is a courtship and finishes with a wedding to the Bride of Christ, which is the church, and they get married and live happily ever afterwards."

We are the Bride of Christ, but what bride doesn't want her complexion to be perfect? What bride doesn't want a white dress—the most beautiful white dress she can get? We are told at the end of the Bible about this wedding and we are told that the Bride has made herself ready, she is wearing fine white linen, which are the righteous deeds of the saints. We are getting ready for the wedding. The more you realise you are the Bride of Christ and where you are heading, the more personal holiness will become an ambition in your life.

Having criticised Augustine once in this chapter, I shall now go back to him and quote him on something that I think is absolutely right. He said this: "He who loves the coming of the Lord is not he who affirms it is far off nor he who says it is near, but rather he who whether it be far or near awaits it with sincere faith, steadfast hope and fervent love." That is how to be ready. Amen.

Chapter 3

THE RETURN OF CHRIST (Part 3)

We are not talking about the immediate future but about the ultimate future and the four things we are talking about are the four certain facts, certain events of the ultimate future. Christians have usually called these the Last Things and that refers to the return of Christ, the Day of Judgment, hell, and heaven. In the next three chapters we are going to look at some rather serious subjects. There are too many Christians today who want to lick the icing off the cake or the jam out of the sandwich. They don't want the more serious side of scripture.

But we come now to the Day of Judgment. My wife and I were in Zurich and we visited Zurich Cathedral. Right above the west door there is a striking stone frieze which had just been painted. It is a frieze of the Day of Judgment. It shows many people being put on the right in white and many being thrown into the flames of hell on the left. In other words, that was put above the west doors so that whenever you go to worship there you are reminded of the Day of Judgment as you go in. It is good to think about it. I told you earlier that the return of Christ is the most frequent prediction in scripture, but the second most frequent is the Day of Judgment.

If I just refer to three texts, that will be enough. Paul,

again speaking in Athens on Mars Hill, said, "God has fixed the day on which he will judge the world in righteousness by a man whom he has appointed." Then we have another of Paul's predictions, in 2 Corinthians chapter five this time, where Paul says, "For we must all appear before the judgment seat of Christ so that each one may receive good or evil according to what he has done in the body." The phrase "in the body" means in this life. Here is another verse from Hebrews chapter nine, a very familiar verse often quoted by preachers: "It is appointed to men to die once and after that comes judgment." In other words, every one of us has two appointments, neither of which we can put in our diary because we don't know the date of either.

One is the day of our death and the other is the day of our judgment. It will not be the same day. In fact, for each individual the day of our death will be a different date and that is the date that will be put on our gravestone, if we have one. But the Day of Judgment is exactly the same date for everyone. So, we each have these two appointments. It is a wise person who thinks about both of them because if you only think about the day of your death that is more likely to make you sin. If you think about both it is more likely to make you refrain from sinning. If you just think about the day that you will die then it can be a case of thinking let's eat, drink, and be merry for tomorrow we die. Let's make the most of every pleasure we can squeeze out of life while we can.

But if you remember that after death comes that second appointment when you are accountable for how you lived here, then that should have quite the opposite effect on the way you live. It is not just numbering our days in quantity but ordering our days in quality that is important. I find on the whole that people are no longer afraid to die. They are more afraid of the process of dying, especially if it is going to be prolonged or painful. But of death itself I meet very few who fear it. They dislike it intensely, they will put it off as long as possible and not talk about it, but I don't meet many who fear death because most people today have stopped believing in that second appointment afterwards.

It is that second appointment that gives us the fear of the first one because the first appointment is the end of an opportunity to get ready for the second. If we don't know the dates, they are not less certain. We need to remember them both, as I have said. But we try to forget both. Why? Because both are profoundly disturbing. It doesn't bring us comfort to think either about the day we die or the day we are going to be judged, yet if you think about it, deep down all of us believe that a day of judgment is absolutely necessary, that it is right.

There is part of us that says there must be a judgment and there are two things that lead us to that feeling. One is the injustice of life; nobody in their right senses could ever say that life is fair or just. One of the first things children learn to say is, "It's not fair." Their faces screw up when they say it and sometimes we go right through life saying it. I was invited to visit a man in hospital who wanted to see a priest. The nearest thing they could find was a Baptist pastor and so I went and said, "What do you want to see a priest about?" He said, "Why has God done this to me?"

I said, "What do you mean what has God done to you?"

He said, "Well, I'm in hospital, aren't I? What have I ever done to deserve this?"

He replied, "Have you never been in hospital before?"

He said, "Never, I've lived a good upright life."

I said, "How old are you?" He said, "Ninety-six."

I said, "You've never been in hospital before?"

"Never. Why should God allow this?"

I said, "How long are you likely to be here?" He said,

"Ten days."

Here he was, this dear old man surrounded by pretty young ladies waiting on his every need. Many men would give their right arm for that and there he was saying, "Why has God done this to me? It's not fair." Now life isn't fair and there is no rational reason why some people suffer so much and other people suffer so little. David had this problem. He wrote a psalm all about it, Psalm 73. He said, "Why do the wicked people prosper? Why do bad people die at a happy old age peacefully in bed?" He said, "I've tried to make my life pure and yet I suffer all day long. Life is purely unjust." It is. In this world it seems to be that the innocent suffer and the wicked get away with it. It is the innocent that are knocked down by hit-and-run drivers, and the guilty are not often found.

The injustice of life demands that some day things will have to be put right so that evil people do not get away with it. The answer of the Bible is there will come a time when injustice will be put right. Nobody will get away with anything. Deep down in us we agree that that should happen. The injustice of life demands it. I was in Palermo in Sicily and that was a city where at the time there were two hundred murders a year. While I was there, forty-one mafia leaders were arrested and put on trial and the jury found them guilty. The judge acquitted all of them. Can you imagine the feelings that were in that city when that happened? People said, "Where is justice?" They just became utterly cynical and lawless themselves because right obviously didn't pay. That is the feeling of so many people. That is the first reason why there has got to be a Day of Judgment in which wrongs are righted and right is vindicated.

But there is another reason why there must be a Day of Judgment and that is the justice of God. It is not just the injustice of life that demands it but the justice of God that demands it. You see, God has allowed so much wrong to be done. He has allowed us to do so much wrong to others. He has allowed it and apparently turned a blind eye to it, but he hasn't. He has taken note of every little thing that has been done. You see, if God never punishes wickedness, he is not a good God. That is why there has to be a Day of Judgment because he is a good God. If he turned a blind eye for all eternity to the things that are being done, we could never call him good. He is also King of the universe. It was part of the function of an ancient king to be the judge, the final court of appeal.

Still to this day all our justice in this country is done in the name of the Queen. It is a function of royalty to be the final court of appeal of justice. God is King and he is the final court of appeal. He is also Judge. Yes, he is Father but he is King and he is Judge. His justice demands that there be a Day of Judgment. God is not mocked, says the Bible. Whatever a man sows that will he also reap. There will come a harvest. There will come a day of reckoning, a day when bills will be paid. God may not judge us every Friday. In fact, I asked one businessman, "Why don't you fear God?" He said, "Because God doesn't press me as hard as my other creditors," which was at least an honest reply.

No, God doesn't press us but one day he will face us—the justice of God demands it. This is a moral universe but why do all have to be judged together on the Day of Judgment? Why does he not judge us at the point of death and decide then, when we die, whether we go to heaven or hell? Why doesn't he do that? Why have we all got to wait even after we die until this day comes up? The answer is really quite simple. If justice is to be done, justice must be *seen* to be done. It is of the essence of justice that it has nothing to hide. It is injustice that has to hide. Therefore, justice must be seen to be done. It is to be public, which is why there

47

is a press bench in every court in this land. In other words, righteousness must be seen to be vindicated.

Therefore, God has appointed a Day of Judgment, a public Day of Judgment when his righteousness will be seen to be done. No one will ever again criticise God for not being fair. There will be three vindications on that day. First of all, God himself will be vindicated. How often have we criticised God for the way he runs the universe? Why does God do this? Why does God allow that? Why did God let my baby die? Why did God let my parents separate when I was a baby? Why, why, why? Whenever we say that we are saying, "God, we can run this universe better than you do." We are actually criticising his providential ways. We are saying, "You're not a very good king. We could do a better job than you do."

God has to be vindicated from all the criticisms that have been made of the way that he has run the universe. One day we will see why he did what he did and when we do we shall understand that he was absolutely right. We shall see with King Nebuchadnezzar, that man who had to go mad for seven years before he saw sense and acknowledged God, but when he did acknowledge God and got his sanity and throne back, he said, "Everything you do, God, is right." One day the whole world will have to come to that conclusion. The whole world will have to be shown that God indeed is vindicated and that everything he did was right, and everything he allowed was right. Indeed, it is part of our Christian hope that one day we will understand the things that we just don't understand now. partly because we are not God and we don't see things his way. But God will do right.

Do you remember Abraham arguing with God about Sodom and his nephew Lot? God said, "Shall I show Abraham what I'm going to do, that I'm going to destroy that city?" He showed Abraham, and Abraham said, "God, supposing there were fifty people who were good in that city, would you destroy them along with the whole city?" God said, "No, I wouldn't."

"Well, supposing there were forty-five good people in that city, would you destroy it?"

"No."

Forty, thirty, twenty, ten. He was trying to protect his nephew Lot, trying to beat God down to saving the city for one man. Do you know what Abraham said to God? "Shall not the judge of all the earth do right?" Crucially, when there are things you can't understand you are really faced with the question of whether your faith believes that God always does right.

When you lost that baby, you couldn't understand why. Do you know God well enough to know that whatever he does is right and whatever he allows is right? Or do you ask why? Do you say, "I wouldn't have let that happen if I'd been God"? Now, on the Day of Judgment God will be seen to have done everything right. What a relief that will be for us. Not only will God be vindicated on the Day of Judgment but Christ will be vindicated. You know what the world thinks of Christ at this moment. Most people don't think he is worth their attention. In fact, they have turned his name into a swear word and you will hear the name Jesus Christ more on the lips of unbelievers than believers today. At places of work, they hit the wrong nail with the hammer and say his name How dare they talk like that about him?

But why do they do it? It is because they are disappointed with him, they are disillusioned with him. They say Christianity has been in the world for two thousand years and what good has it done? People think Gandhi has done more for the world than Jesus did. But one day Jesus will be vindicated. The last time the world saw Jesus they saw him naked and dying on a cross. But on the Day of Judgment, they will see him vindicated and every knee shall bow and every tongue confess that he is Lord. Then God's people will be vindicated on that day. How Christians have suffered. I was shattered to find out how many Christians died last year for Jesus. Do you know how many Christian martyrs there were this year [Editor: at the time when the author was speaking]? If I said three thousand would you be amazed? If I said thirty thousand would you think I was going crazy? If I said three hundred thousand what would you think?

Well, I have gone one too high in that last figure. The estimated figure I have seen is two hundred and eighty-six thousand people who died for Jesus last year. There has not been one year for two millennia during which people have not died because they loved the Lord. The world has dismissed them. The world was not worthy. But on the Day of Judgment God's people will be vindicated. All those who suffered for him will be vindicated. Justice will be done and be seen to be done and be acknowledged by all. So that is why there has got to be a Day of Judgment.

Yet in spite of all this, there is something in us that dislikes the whole idea. Or to put it more honestly, we like the idea of Day of Judgment for everyone else as long as we are excused. What we blame others for we excuse in ourselves. We want to see them punished for the things we do. Isn't it extraordinary, this perverted outlook of ours? Of course, science has given us two excuses for what we do. It has given us the excuses of heredity and environment. The science of biology says that we are the product of our genes. The sciences of psychology and sociology are able to say it is the way we were brought up. Look, it has become almost the "in" thing now to say, "I'm not a sinner. I'm a victim. I'm a patient. I need healing not forgiveness."

I have sat through many court cases and found that at a certain stage the best way to try to get a man off was to get a psychiatrist to plead that he wasn't responsible for his actions, that he was the victim of the way he had been treated. Then, of course, he can be given treatment rather than punishment. We went through a phase where many judges were impressed with that plea. To those I have tried to help through court I have said, "Take your responsibility. Be a man." You see, every one of us is the result of the choices we have made. Did you know that everybody over forty is responsible for their face?

Now, perhaps you are someone who can afford to laugh at that, but others won't be able to do so. If you are over forty and you don't like what you see in the mirror every morning you know who is to blame. Up to forty you have got the features that you were born with. but over forty you have got the expression that you have given yourself. You are responsible for what you have become. I remember one man in the dock saying to the judge, "Your honour, I got into bad company." I noticed he didn't say, "I chose the wrong friends." "I got into bad company" or I fell into bad company as if he couldn't help it. We know too many people who have risen far above their background or fallen far below it to say that it is a decisive factor. The real factor in the formation of our character is the choices we have made through life. You and I are the result of those choices and the Day of Judgment will reveal our responsibility. Let me say absolutely categorically that you have nothing to fear if you fear being blamed for something you are not responsible for. God will never blame you for something you couldn't help—never. But that is not what worries me.

What worries me are the things that I could have helped. So, you have nothing to fear about a miscarriage of justice on the Day of Judgment—nothing. God will never blame anyone for something they were not responsible for. But he will blame us for those things we are responsible for, as we shall see, the things that we didn't do and not just the things that we did. A little child said to the teacher at school, "Teacher, you wouldn't punish me for something I hadn't done, would you?"

The teacher said, "No, of course not." "Well, I haven't done my homework," said the child! There are sins of omission as well as sins of commission.

We have the Anglican prayer "and the things that we have done that we ought not to have done and the things we have not done that we ought to have done". The real fear is not for those who say, "I'm not really wicked," but for those who say, "I know I really am." The older you get the greater that fear comes because the older you get the more you know yourself and the more you realise what you are really like. Basically, we are terribly self-centred creatures.

Our first concern is usually our own feelings, our second concern after that is other people's feelings, and the last concern of all is God's feelings. There are many people who have no idea that God has feelings too. Yet the Bible is full of God's feelings. I hope you have a Bible that distinguishes poetry from prose. In the Bible, prose looks like a newspaper column, with the print going right to the sides. But in poetry the words are printed in shorter lines with gaps between. You know the difference. I hope you have a Bible that does that because there is a very important reason why sometimes God speaks to us in prose and sometimes in poetry. When he speaks in prose, he is communicating his thoughts from his mind to your mind through the prose. But when he is communicating his feelings from his heart to your heart he uses poetry. Well, we do the same when we are in love and we write poetry because we want to express feelings rather than thoughts. The Bible is packed with God's feelings. We find out the things that make him sad, the things that make him happy, the things that make him feel sick, the things that make him angry. The Day of Judgment is very much connected with God's anger. There are two words for anger in the New Testament. One is for that slow, simmering anger that goes in and doesn't come out. It goes in and it goes deep and it is long. The other word is for a quick, short temper that boils over quickly and is usually over quite soon.

Now, I wonder which your problem is? Is your problem the slow, simmering anger inside? People don't even know you are angry but you are. Or do you have the quick anger? Perhaps you have both. Which do you think is God's anger, the slow or the quick? Well, the answer is both. If I can use an illustration, have you ever put a pan of milk on the stove and then got occupied with your visitors or someone else and suddenly you find the thing has boiled over?

If only you had stayed and watched it that wouldn't have happened because you would have seen the first bubbling. You would have seen that simmering and you would have had it off the heat as quickly as you could before it exploded. But when your attention is off that simmering it seems so quick until it is all over the stove and you have got to clean it all up. Now, God's anger at the moment is simmering. That is why many people do not notice it. It is there and all the symptoms are there that God's anger is upon us. If you read Romans 1, you will find a description of what happens in society when God is angry with it, revealing his simmering anger. It doesn't show too much in great disasters but it shows in other things. It shows particularly in the way that people develop uncontrollable appetites, so that food and sex become obsessions.

When God is angry with a society, people develop not only uncontrollable appetites but also unnatural relationships, particularly homosexual relationships. It is all there in Romans 1. That is what happens to their bodies when God's anger is on a society. What happens to their minds is that they develop anti-social behaviour. There is a list in Romans 1, that could have been taken off any police desk blotter, of anti-social attitudes, rebellion against authority and disobedience to parents. There is a whole long list there of rebellious attitudes, which lead to a violent society, a lawless attitude.

Now, if these are the symptoms of God's simmering anger, he would be a bold man who would claim that God is not angry with Britain today. The signs are there for people who look but most people don't even think that God has feelings and, therefore, they don't notice the simmering anger. But the concept in the New Testament of the Day of Judgment is that it is the day when the anger of God boils over. It is called the day of his anger or the day of his wrath. It is the day when, finally, his anger so explodes that people know he is angry, whether they noticed it earlier or not.

That is an interesting insight into the Day of Judgment: the day when God's anger shows. We are even told that on that day people will cry out to the mountains, "Fall on us," rather than face the expression on the face of God and his Son Jesus. People are then saying, "Save us, fall on us so that we don't see the wrath of the Lamb and of God." Can you imagine a situation in which people would rather be crushed in an earthquake than face the anger of those two persons, Father and Son? It is a sobering description. Now, Romans 1 leads to Romans 2 and the latter tells us a great deal about this day of his wrath and says that we are to notice his present anger and deal with it now or deal with the cause of it now so that we are not storing up his anger for the day when it boils over.

Here are some of the things that Romans 2 tells us. First, the Day of Judgment is for everybody, without any exception. All human beings who have ever lived are going to be resurrected. Resurrection is not just for the righteous, it is for the wicked as well. Everybody is going to get that new body. Following the resurrection of all, the judgment of all will take place. It won't matter whether you were great or small, high or low, whether you were well known and famous or nobody knew you. Each person will be dealt with personally. You will not have anyone to stand by your side on that day. You will not be able to hide behind anybody on that day. You will stand alone.

That is one of the clearest teachings of scripture, that even though we will all be together on that day, each of us will be dealt with entirely separately, separate from our relatives, separate from our friends—alone. So, first it will be for everybody. Second, as I have mentioned, we are told that Jesus will be the Judge, not the Father. The human Jesus will be the judge. I am not sure that that comforts me greatly because if there was one person who could see right through people it was Jesus. He knew everything that went on inside people's hearts. Thirdly, what kind of evidence will be looked at in the judgment? What kind of evidence will determine whether we are acquitted or found guilty?

Well, let me tell you what the evidence will *not* be. Firstly, the evidence will not be your appearance. It will not be how you have appeared to other people because, frankly, most of us can fool others, not maybe all the time but you can fool other people by your appearance. You can put on a front and you can hide your feelings. You can put a privet hedge up outside and lace curtains inside. But on that day appearance will matter not at all because God does not look at the outward appearance.

Secondly, the evidence will not be your profession. There are many people who profess to love the Lord, many people who profess faith, many people who say, "Lord, did we not cast out demons in your name?" All that is profession but on the Day of Judgment what we profess will be totally irrelevant. What we say about ourselves will not be considered. Thirdly, the evidence will not be our reputation. We won't be able to say, "Well, Jesus, just talk to so and so. They have a different opinion about me." Reputation will matter not a bit on that day. So, what will be the evidence? The answer is two things: our deeds and our words; what we have done and what we have said.

The Bible says that if you have never said the wrong thing you are absolutely perfect, so there is a very good test for you to apply as to how sanctified you are. I wonder how many of us would be happy if there were a big screen and everything we had done had been filmed and was now being shown to everybody else. Or supposing if everything we had said, even in private, had been recorded and was being played to everybody. I wonder how many friends we would be left with! Jesus said that for every idle word we will be brought into judgment. That is quite a thought. The idle words are those that slip out when we are not controlling our tongue properly, those that slip out when we are overtired or when we are angry. For every idle word we will be brought into judgment.

This is the evidence and God is absolutely fair. He has no favourites whatsoever. I suppose one of the most serious things that Jesus said about the Day of Judgment was this: It will be the day on which the secrets of men will be judged. He put it another way when he said that what has been whispered in the bed chamber will be shouted from the housetops, the day on which the secrets of men will be judged, not the things that the world saw but the things that only God was aware of. Well, I told you it wasn't a comfortable subject!

The next thing that we are told is that this God is so fair and so just that he will only judge people by the light they have received, and this is the answer to all those queries about those who have never heard. How often people have said to me, "Well, what about those who've never heard

about Jesus?" I say, "Do you want to become a missionary?"
I find that those who keep asking me about those who have
never heard do not want to go and tell them. They are only
trying to find fault with Christianity. They have no real
intention of going to share the good news with those who
have never heard. But the answer of the Bible is absolutely
clear: those who have never heard will not be condemned
for never having heard. In fact, Paul said quite clearly that
those who have only heard the Ten Commandments will
only be judged by the Ten Commandments.

Those who have never heard the Ten Commandments
will be judged only by what their conscience has told them
is right and wrong. Now is that fair? It is absolutely fair.
God will only judge by the light that has been received. The
problem is that everybody has received some light and in
two particular ways, says Paul: they have received light from
their conscience within and from the creation outside. From
the creation outside they must know that there is a greater
power than themselves and from their conscience from
within they must know that that power is a moral power and
is concerned with right and wrong. So, all a person needs to
do to be acquitted before God is to say, "God, I have always
done what my conscience told me was right." That's all, but
who can? That is the problem. You see, every single person
on earth has a concept of right and wrong. The Bible says
that is God writing his law in their inner heart.

The proof that everybody has a conscience is that they are
jolly quick to tell other people when they are wrong. Have
you ever noticed that? If God only judged you for what
you said was wrong in other people that would be enough,
wouldn't it? But we are so quick to condemn in others what
we have done ourselves. Indeed, psychology tells us that we
are more ready to criticise in others what we either do or want
to do ourselves. So those brought up in Christian countries

will be judged by the light they have received. Those brought up in the Jewish faith will be judged by the light they have received. Those brought up as pagans will be judged by the light they have received. All have received light.

This is why there are degrees of punishment in the Bible and why it is more tolerable for Sodom and Gomorrah than Capernaum because Sodom and Gomorrah never had Jesus and never saw his miracles but Capernaum did. Though Sodom and Gomorrah have disappeared off the face of the earth so have Capernaum and Bethsaida and Chorazin, but they had much greater light and they were judged by that light. So, God will never judge you for what you didn't know or for the light you never received. The problem is that every one of us has had enough light to know that right is right and wrong is wrong. So, what is the verdict going to be on that day? There can only be one. Everybody is guilty. It is the only verdict that there could possibly be.

So why go through the whole rigmarole of the Day of Judgment just to find everybody guilty when all those books are opened? I often found the programme *This is Your Life* to be very interesting. There was once a man on *This is Your Life* whom I knew personally and whom I knew was a crook. He was an employee of my grandparents and I knew what he was like. Yet on this *This is Your Life* programme he was a hero; he was a saint. It was most uncomfortable sitting there watching and if you read the articles that are written about that programme you know they discover all kinds of horrible things. The researchers really dig it out and then they censor it carefully and pick out all the nice bits.

Be in no doubt, one day a book will be opened: this is your life and there is everything in that book, not just the nice bits, not just what other people have thought of you or seen. There is everything there. How will you feel? Well, I have got good news for you because there is another book that will be opened on the Day of Judgment. It is called the Lamb's Book of Life. It is a book full of the names of bad people but they have all become relatives of Jesus. They have been written in his book under his name and can be acquitted because he lived the only perfect life that has ever been lived and my name is under his in that book. That is the only hope I will have on that day.

I am going to point out in the next chapter that I am afraid you can get your name blotted out of that book. But if your name stays in that book and is there on the Day of Judgment then you are acquitted. Isn't that amazing? I am going to tell you why that is possible later in this book. That is the only hope for me or for you or for anyone else, that on that day when those books are opened and the book, "*This is my life*" is opened. The only hope I will have will be that my name will still be in that other book. If my name is in that book it will be under Jesus' name and covered by his life, not mine. Then God will be able to acquit me. Well, I think it is healthy to think about the Day of Judgment.

It is healthy to remind people that we all have these two appointments, the first on the day we die and following that the day when we all stand together before Jesus and give an account of how we lived down here. What lies beyond that day? Well, there are only two possibilities since there are only two possible verdicts, guilty or innocent, and we are going to be looking in the next two chapters at what happens to the guilty and then we shall finish up with what happens to the acquitted.

Chapter 4

THE PUNISHMENT OF HELL (Part 1)

I once preached to a congregation of dogs—mostly the Labrador breed—and they gave me incredible attention. Do you believe me? It was a guest service and each of the dogs had brought a guest who was blind. Oh, now you believe me? You should have believed me the first time! It was the annual Torch Trust rally for the blind and a lot of them had brought their guide dogs and blind people usually listen to you with their head tilted to one side but the dogs listened and they watched this man waving his arms about. When I looked at the congregation all I could see were these dogs' eyes looking at me. That morning I asked the Lord what I should preach about to these blind people. He said, "Preach about hell."

I thought, "I can't do that—they're handicapped, they've suffered, they need a word of comfort and encouragement," but the Lord said, "Preach about hell." So, I talked about a verse in the Sermon on the Mount: "It is better to lose your sight and enter into life than to keep your eyes and go to hell." I said, "Do you blind people ever pray for those of us who are sighted, because most of our temptations come through our eyes?" It is called "the lust of the eyes". There was an elderly lady there—eighty-four I believe she was—and she had been blind from birth and had never been able to see. She was very resentful and bitter about this.

But for the first time in her whole life, she felt pity for me because I could see, and all the bitterness left her heart and she opened her heart to the Lord, and on the bus back that day she sang hymns all the way. She died the following Thursday, and the first person she ever saw was Jesus. It was not the first time I had preached on hell but I have not done it frequently. Have you noticed that very few are doing so these days? It seems to have dropped right out. In fact, if you want to hear the word again go and work among unbelievers and you will hear it all the time. It is being treated simply as an expletive now—one way in which people try to take the edge off it and take the fear away, to use the word so frequently that it loses its meaning.

Have you ever heard about Charlie "Dry Hole" Woods? I am sure you haven't, but Charlie Woods got the nickname "Dry Hole" because he was always digging for oil in his backyard without finding any. That was until he actually found the biggest gusher in California and it yielded something like eighteen thousand barrels a day and at its peak it got up to eighty-five thousand barrels and nobody teased Charlie Woods any more. But after he got the first gusher of this black stuff pouring out he was being interviewed by a reporter and this is what he said to the reporter: "It's hell, literally hell. It roars like hell. It mounts, surges, and sweeps like hell. It is as uncomfortable as hell and as uncontrollable as hell. It's black and hot as hell," which is rather overdoing the word, don't you think?

When you use the word as freely as that it no longer instils fear. It no longer means what it originally meant. That is one way in which the world is laughing it off. The second way in which the world laughs off the idea of hell is to make it a subject of comedy. It is quite a tribute to the communication of the church that most people outside know what the word hell means and it is quite amazing how many jokes comedians make about hell, about its temperature, about the company there, about all kinds of things. That is another way in which the edge has been taken off it and people no longer fear it. Hell has also been reinterpreted in an existential way. I mean by this that people say, "You make your hell on earth." Have you heard that phrase? Well, of course, that does two things.

First of all, it brings hell to this side of death so it is not to be feared beyond death. It also means that no longer does God make the decision, or the Lord Jesus make the decision, to send people to hell; they do it for themselves. So, if you go there it is your decision, not his. Again, in a very subtle way the edge has been taken off it. That is how the general public talk about hell. What is amazing is that the church inside has stopped talking about it. It seems to have disappeared. We are going to see in a moment that the serious side of that is that many preachers, even evangelical preachers, no longer believe in it, even though Jesus apparently did.

So, we have got quite a serious subject before us. People have an aversion to the doctrine of hell. I am not surprised. It is the most offensive and disturbing doctrine in the Christian faith. I wish I didn't have to include it but I am talking about those things in the future that are absolutely certain and this is one of those four things about which we can be absolutely sure. Hell is real. If it is not then Jesus was a liar and I am not prepared to say that. Arguments have been used against hell, even within the church. I am talking about the church now and believers. Arguments are being used by scholars and theologians to argue hell out of existence. They usually do it by taking one attribute of God and making that the whole of God and then arguing from this that hell cannot possibly coexist with it.

The glory of God is the sum of all his attributes and it is very dangerous to take any one of those attributes and make that the foundation of your thinking. Let me explain what I mean. Some people take the love of God, which is one of his attributes, and they make it the whole and, therefore, they say, "How could a God of love send anyone to hell?" As much as to argue, if I loved people, I couldn't do that to them. How can God love people and do that to them? Others have highlighted God's power and they say, "If God is all-powerful then he cannot fail in what he sets his mind to. Therefore, if he sets his mind to getting everyone to heaven, he can achieve that. His power is able to do it. Therefore, if anyone finishes up in hell then God has failed. He is weak and his power is not omnipotent. His power is inadequate to save everybody."

Then there are those who take his justice and say, "Is it just to punish for all eternity a few years of vice or crime? Is it fair that people like Saddam Hussein and my nice next-door neighbour finish up in the same place?" So, they take God's justice and argue from that against hell. Now all these are doing exactly the same thing. They are taking part of God's character and making it the whole. But each of his attributes qualifies the others and they all blend together. In other words, God is not just love, he is holy love. That makes a big difference. His holiness qualifies his love and however much he loves us his holiness cannot allow sin to go on forever, so that his love is qualified by his holiness. His power is qualified by his love.

He will not force anyone to go to heaven. He doesn't want people in heaven who are there involuntarily. He wants people freely to choose to be in his family and that qualifies his power. He could make us all be good but he has chosen not to because he wants sons and daughters and not robots in glory. So, all these are arguing from part of God instead of from the whole of God. That is a mistake that many Christians make. They see the nice side and they don't like the other side but the New Testament says, "Behold then the goodness and the severity of God." They belong together and to get a big view of God you need the whole counsel of God and the whole truth. So, what do these theologians and scholars who are arguing against hell as incompatible with at least part of God's character propose to put in its place? What are the alternatives that are being preached today?

There are two main ones. We could go through a whole lot but there are two big ones that are being widely preached today. One is an alternative to hell that is being preached by those we call liberals, who do not accept the total inspiration and authority of scripture. Alas, the other alternative is now being preached by those who do accept the inspiration and authority of scripture, believe it or not. So, what are the two alternatives? I am sorry to give you two rather big words now and they both end in "ism". Always beware of words that end with the three letters I-S-M because most of the words that end in "ism" have a demonic power to become an obsession with people, even when they are religious "isms".

Anglicanism and Methodism and baptism and evangelism are the only isms I am happy with. But, apart from those, beware of every ism because they have this capacity to obsess a person. Here are the two isms that are being proposed in place of hell. Number one is *universalism*. Now, this is the liberal alternative to hell and universalists believe that some day somehow, everybody will end up in heaven. It involves believing that after death there will be a second chance and a third and a fourth and a fifth, indeed an indefinite number of opportunities to be saved, so that people may decide later to go to heaven even if they did not decide before they died. Of course, if you find yourself in hell you have got a real incentive to choose heaven. So that is universalism.

Actually, universalism has two forms, one of which says, "One day everybody *will be* saved." But there is a modern version of it that says, "Everybody is *already* saved. Since Jesus died for the world everybody has been saved and all we need to do is tell them that they are saved." A pope committed himself to this view that all people have been redeemed by Christ whether they believe it or not. They are all on their way to heaven. The task of the church is to tell them that they are going there and to tell them they are saved. That is the good news.

Neither of these forms of universalism has any room for hell at all. Either we are all going to be saved or we already have been saved but either way everybody is heading for heaven. That is the universal bit of the universalism. Now, evangelicals who believe in the inspiration and authority of the Bible cannot, of course, accept that because the Bible makes it quite clear that there will be a division on the Day of Judgment between the saved and the lost, between the guilty and the acquitted. There is a black and white division in scripture and between those on the broad way that leads to destruction and those on the narrow way that leads to life. You can't get around this division in the human race in scripture.

So, what is the alternative to hell being preached by leading evangelicals in this country? The answer is *annihilationism*. This is the belief that sinners simply cease to be. They go into oblivion. They don't suffer in hell. They become nothing. Again, there are two versions of this. One is to believe that sinners become nothing at the moment of death while the other is to believe that sinners become nothing after the Day of Judgment. Appeal is made to some parts of scripture—for example, that hell is fire that destroys. You can't survive in fire, which means that eternal punishment does not refer to the eternal suffering but the eternal effect of being annihilated.

Well, I would have thought it was pretty eternal to be annihilated but that is how they get around the phrase, "eternal punishment," that it is eternal in its effect but not in its experience. This is now a hot debate. You have seen it in magazines. Perhaps you saw in one national Christian magazine a lady writing a letter who just said, "I could not love a God who would send anyone to hell." That is where she stood. That was what she said.

Well, frankly, it is saying that Jesus didn't know what he was talking about, because we know everything we know about hell from the lips of Jesus. Did you know that? God didn't trust anybody else to tell us such a terrible truth. We don't know about it from John or Paul or Peter. There is not a word about hell in the Old Testament. Everything we know comes from the lips of Jesus himself and yet if there was anyone who knew God well it was surely his Son. He knew all about God's love and God's power and God's justice and yet still he taught hell. So, we turn to the teaching of Jesus and before I look at it in detail, I want to explain something. I want to give you a framework of thinking, which you need before you can understand the rest of what I am going to affirm.

This is the framework. Human existence is in three phases, three stages, not two. It is a very common idea even inside the church that you die and you go to heaven or hell. That is based on a framework of two phases, but from what I have already taught about the Day of Judgment you know that there are three phases of human existence. Phase number one is the one that we are all in right now. That is this world in which I am an embodied spirit. At death, my spirit and body will be separated and I will be finished with my body. It will only have been an overcoat that I have worn. My second phase of existence will be that of a disembodied spirit. I have never been that so it is going to be a new experience and, like Paul, I am not quite sure about it at this stage, and yet equally I am with Paul sure that it will be far better than this life with a body.

But Paul did say, "I'd rather go straight from phase one to phase three, from my old body to my new body," but even so, "if I have to be unclothed," as he put it, "I'd rather be absent from the body and present with the Lord, which is far better." So, phase two is where you are absent from the body. If you know the Lord, you are present with the Lord. It is almost irrelevant to ask where that will be because without a body you don't ask where. You don't need to be located, as it were. Spirits are not subject to the same dimensional existence as bodies are.

The important thing is who will you be with. You will be with the Lord, fully conscious and able to communicate, but without a body. Phase three comes later when we all, together, get a new body and become again embodied spirits and full human beings in the total sense. Now do you realise that Jesus went through all these three phases himself in less than a week? On the day he died his body and his spirit separated and he gave up his spirit to the Father who gave it. For the next three days and nights he was fully conscious and fully active and preaching to those who were drowned in the days of Noah's Flood. We know that from Simon Peter, who has told us in his letter. I imagine that Jesus told Peter this when he met him on the first Easter Sunday. We don't know where they met or what was said, we just know that he appeared to Peter. What an extraordinary titbit of information. It seems to me proof that nobody invented the Bible. Who would have thought that up? So, Jesus was fully conscious. fully communicating. But more than that, the people who had drowned in Noah's flood were fully conscious.

Two minutes after you have died you will be fully conscious. You will know who you are. You will be able to communicate. If you are with the Lord, how exciting that will be. Somebody asked me after I said that, "What about one minute after you're dead?" Okay, one minute, one second after you are dead, you will be fully conscious. You won't go into oblivion. Jesus didn't. But you will go into that disembodied phase. Heaven and hell belong to the third phase. That is what I want to get across now. They are both places for people with bodies. That is very important. I don't use the phrase "go to heaven". I'll tell you more in the last chapter. But this talking about going to heaven or hell when you die is quite misleading. Nobody is in hell yet, not even Satan. It is an uninhabited place. It is interesting that Jesus spoke of both heaven and hell with the same word.

He said that both are being "prepared". "I go to prepare a place for you" and "Depart from me, you cursed, into the everlasting punishment prepared for the devil and his angels." Both heaven and hell are at the moment in a state of preparation. They are not yet inhabited. So, I prefer to say that somebody who died in faith has gone to be with the Lord, which is how the New Testament talks—not where they are but who they are with is the important thing in that middle phase. So, have you got this framework, the threefold phases? The Bible tells us very little about the middle phase. It concentrates our thinking on the final phase beyond the resurrection and the judgment. That is the hell I am talking about, not something in between. I am talking about that beyond the resurrection.

That is what Jesus talked about and I want to look at how he described it first. Now, I suppose we all have a mental picture of hell. Usually, we have picked it up from some bad experience we have had, and two experiences come back to my mind whenever I hear the word "hell". The first was when I was in Hong Kong with a lady called Jackie Pullinger. You may have heard of her experiences in the walled city of Hong Kong. She took me into the walled city.

The first surprise was there was no wall. I imagined this big stone wall but it was torn down by the Japanese during the war and thrown into the harbour to make the runway for the aircraft. When you land in a jumbo jet, you are landing on the wall of the walled city but the walled city itself was still there when I went and it was a pile of shanty houses fifteen or twenty storeys high, just piled on top of each other. It was a tiny bit of Hong Kong that was not owned by the British. It was not owned by anybody. Therefore, in that tiny part of the city, which can't be much more than ten times the size of a church, there was no law, there were no police. You could do anything you liked in that city. You can imagine that crime and vice flourished. It was where the triads had their headquarters. It was where the pimps and prostitutes lived. It was where the drug dealers lived. It could not be touched.

It was going to have to be pulled down before Hong Kong was handed back to China. You went in through a little opening and the place was so dark inside. If you were visiting someone on the top floor you had to climb up on someone else's roof. The filth, the sewage, the rats – it was indescribable. The only bright room in it was right in the middle on the ground floor, the room where Jackie Pullinger prays for drug addicts. She is an amazing lady. When I came out into the sunlight after being in that horrid, dark, dismal, depressing place full of vice and crime, instinctively I said, "I've just been to hell." That was years ago but about three years after that I experienced something worse.

I was in Poland and I went to a place called Auschwitz. There I stood in a bare, windowless chamber. It had two doors, with one at one end and another at the other. There were what looked like shower heads in the ceiling, but through those shower heads came the deadly Zyklon B gas that put hundreds and hundreds to death. They used to force men, women, and children into that room two hundred and fifty at a time. They couldn't move. They were told they were going to have a shower so they left their clothes outside and then they were gassed. Then they cut their hair off to stuff cushions, pulled the gold out of their teeth with pliers. If they had tattoos on their skin, they carefully took them off to make lampshades. They melted their fat down to make soap, then they burned the bodies to ashes and sold it off as fertiliser. From coming into the camp to be sold out as fertiliser took one and a half hours. I stood alone in that chamber. I felt I was in hell. Interestingly, I remember opening my paper after Princess Anne had been to Auschwitz and that was her title as well: *Princess in Hell*. Well, we have all got our pictures, our experiences, and yet none of them really is like the picture Jesus gave us.

Let us go to Jesus. How did he think of hell? The answer is really quite simple. He thought of hell as a rubbish dump, a garbage dump. He always called it Gehenna and that is Hebrew for the Valley of Hinnom. That is a real valley. It is just outside the city of Jerusalem, but tourists never see it. One reason is that it is too deep and when you are in the old city of Jerusalem you are just not aware of the valley. You have to go out of the south gate and look down to see it. It goes right down so deep and so dark that the sun doesn't touch one part of the bottom of the valley. When I first went to Israel in 1961 that valley was still being used for the same purpose as in Jesus' day.

The smoke was rising out of it and here was all the rubbish from the city being incinerated, and I went down into the valley. The rotten food was there and the maggots were there. The picture was there and Jesus said, "Where the fire never goes out and the worms never die." So Gehenna was that valley. But you can't see it now because it has been landscaped. It is now a public park in a beautiful valley but you can still go and walk through it. It is just outside the city. The gate on the south wall is, significantly, called the Dung Gate and you can guess why. It is where they took all the sewage and tipped it into the valley. All the rubbish went down there and it was just kept burning to try to keep it low. That was what it always had been.

But way, way back in the Old Testament period that valley had some very sinister associations. It was down in the bottom of that valley that God's own people Israel worshipped a horrible pagan demonic entity called Moloch who demanded human sacrifice, and there down at the bottom of that valley they burned alive their own babies to Moloch. If you read Jeremiah, he said, "This valley will be called a valley of desolation." From then on it became the rubbish dump of the city, a horrible place. Now it has some other associations too. A crucified criminal was never buried. His body was taken off the cross and thrown into the Valley of Gehenna for the maggots to eat and the birds to pick at.

That might have happened to our Lord Jesus had Joseph of Arimathea not come forward and said, "Have my tomb." Jesus might have finished up in Gehenna but for Joseph. One of the twelve disciples did finish up there. Judas hanged himself and he put a rope over a tree at the top of the cliff overlooking the Valley of Hinnom and threw himself off and the rope broke and his body tumbled down and it says in crude language, "His bowels gushed out when he hit the bottom." It became known as the Field of Blood and if you ask the Israeli guide, he will show you the field of blood at the bottom of that valley. That is the valley we are talking about.

It is the valley where all the rubbish is thrown, where everything useless is thrown, where everything dirty is thrown to get rid of it. Jesus said, "If you want a picture of hell just go out of the south gate and look down." That is my idea of hell. It brings to vivid light the word "perish" because the word "perish" does not mean to cease to be. It means to cease to be useful. If you have got a hot water bottle that has perished, has it ceased to be? No, it still looks like a hot water bottle. The only trouble is you cannot use it as a hot water bottle because it has perished and that is the literal meaning of the word "perish" in scripture. It doesn't mean to be annihilated. It means to be ruined.

When a woman poured ointment all over Jesus, Judas Iscariot said, "That ointment is perished." It is useless now; It has been wasted. It is said of the prodigal son that he was wasted, that he was perished, that he was ruined, lost. That is the word for lost. Here is the greatest tragedy that can ever happen to a human being, that a person made in the image of God, made to serve God's purposes has so perished that God says: "I can't use that person any more. They are rubbish in my universe." The phrase "go to hell" is not in scripture. The phrase that Jesus always used was, "Thrown into hell," because that is precisely what you do with rubbish, isn't it? You always throw it away. That is the verb that is always used— "thrown" into.

Jesus was very careful to say that your body and soul would be ruined in hell—not just your soul but your body. That is why I have said: "Hell is a place for people with bodies," therefore, it is not a place where you go to when you die but a place you go to after resurrection. So that is what Jesus' picture was, a picture of a rubbish dump for people who have wasted. Just to slip in a little good news, God is in the recycling business. That is what *salvation* means.

Too many people think *saved* means *safe*. It doesn't. I'll show you that in the next chapter. It means salvaged, and salvaged is the nearest English equivalent to salvation and it means to take rubbish and recycle it and make it useful again. Now there is an intriguing little letter in the New Testament written to a man called Philemon about a slave called Onesimus. Do you know what Onesimus means? Onesimus means useful. Isn't that amazing? That slave called Useful ran away from home, found his way to Rome where he thought he could hide, made the biggest mistake of his life, met up with Paul, and got converted. Paul says, "You've got to go back to your master." "Oh, but he'll kill me. I ran away." "No, I know him. He's a Christian. I will write a letter to cover you."

Paul wrote that lovely letter and said, "If he took any of your money, I'll pay it back. But listen, he really has become useful again. He has been recycled. You found him useless but you will find him Onesimus now." A lovely pun in that little letter and it is a picture of redemption. It is precisely what Jesus has done with all of us. He is sending us back to God and saying, "He's useful again, Father. She's useful again. She was no use to you, she was running away from you, he was running away from you, but I've recycled them." That is what salvation is, to be recycled so that rubbish doesn't finish up in the rubbish dump but becomes useful to God again. What a picture that is.

Jesus not only described hell but he also gave us a very clear understanding of what it would be like to experience it. I just want to finish this chapter by telling you five things he said hell would be like to experience. First, he said, it will be a place of intense physical discomfort. For one thing, there will be no natural light there, total darkness. You may have your eyes but you won't see anything because there will be no light there at all. He kept calling it "outer darkness". He said it is going to be a very thirsty place where you will beg for a drop of water. That is because it will be a very hot place with extreme heat, which is one of the most unpleasant experiences we have.

He also said it would be a very smelly place. Sulphur is an element in most of the worst smells there are. Decaying, putrefaction is one of the worst smells on earth. Physical discomfort and a place of mental depression. It is strange that Jesus said there will be weeping and gnashing of teeth because those seem to be contradictory. Weeping is sorrow and gnashing of teeth is anger. How can you have sorrow and anger at the same time? The answer is very simple. They both come together in frustration and when you know the chances you did have and the chances you missed and you can never have them back again there is a mixture of self-pity and sorrow and anger with yourself and anger with God. This strange weeping and gnashing of teeth that Jesus mentioned points to this mental depression.

It is a place of moral depravity. Can you imagine having to live forever with people who are totally depraved, who lost all image of God, who are behaving like animals, a place where every vice and crime is practised, a place where you have to live with it all, a place of utter moral depravity? No goodness there at all. No patience, no kindness, no love. I wonder whether people realise that when you choose to live without God you choose to live without goodness at the same time because all the good things that human beings are capable of come from God. It is part of his image still left in us and when that image is totally perished that is the bit that goes. Therefore, it will be a place of social depravity.

You can be in the middle of a huge crowd and be totally lonely, right? Now, why are you lonely in a crowd? It is when you feel that nobody takes any interest in you, nobody cares for you, and nobody loves you. You can be surrounded by thousands of people but if nobody cares for you or loves you, you can feel desperately alone. I believe everybody in hell will feel that social deprivation because, once again, it is only God who has made love possible, and neither family love nor friendship will be there. Therefore, finally, it will be a place of utter spiritual desolation. There will be no prayer there. What is the point of praying if there is no God to hear you? There will be no worship there. What would be the point of worshipping when there is nobody to worship?

You see, the worst thing about hell is that you have to live without God. Now, people say, "Well, that's not so bad, I'm living without him now." No, you are not. In this world, nobody is living without God. His Spirit is still touching people, still pleading, still restraining them from being as bad as they really are. But look, when God takes the brakes off, we don't go uphill, we go downhill. We see what happens when God takes his hands off when we look at Romans 1. It says there that men gave God up. So what did God do? God gave man up and the results were pretty horrifying. You see, if God gave you up totally you would not be a better person, you would be a very much worse person than you are. None of us knows how much restraint there has been in our life through the influence of parents or friends that have held us back from doing what we might have done. Sometimes you discover your real self when the restraints come off and when you are away from home and nobody knows where you are. That is when you find out who you really are. That is what hell will be like—spiritual deadness. Nobody will ever have a thought about spiritual things. That is what we choose if we choose to live without God. We cannot get away from God here, but God can get right away from us in that third phase of our existence. There are other things to say about hell, but that is enough for now.

Chapter 5

THE PUNISHMENT OF HELL (Part 2)

Continuing with this sombre subject, I particularly want to address this very serious question: how long will hell last? You see, even some annihilationists, who believe we are heading for oblivion if we are sinners, believe that we go to hell for a little bit of suffering before we are obliterated. Frankly, all this means is that annihilation is good news. Perhaps that is why those who believe this don't preach this, because it would have the wrong effect on people. But actually, if I am a sinner and I have sinned for seventy or eighty years, and got away with it, oblivion is great news, isn't it? Even if I am sent to hell for a bit there is still the good news, there is the hope of being obliterated. So, in fact, annihilation is good news.

But let us look at this. How long does anyone suffer in hell? The traditional answer has always been "forever". But that answer is being very widely questioned, I have to say, mainly by Anglican evangelicals right now. But what does Jesus say? I think the whole question is being approached from the wrong angle. The angle from which most of the discussion is taking place today is, "How long will human beings suffer in hell?" Whereas I believe we have got to approach that question from another angle. You see, hell was never prepared for human beings. God never intended any human beings to go there. "He prepared it," says Jesus, "for the devil and all his angels." He didn't prepare it for us.

In the sheep and the goats parable—it is not a parable really, it is a prophecy—in that story, Jesus says to the goats, "Depart from me you cursed into the everlasting punishment prepared for the devil and his angels." God prepares heaven for us but he prepared hell for the devil and his angels, whom we call demons. That is about a third of the angels in existence who have sided with Satan and rebelled against God according to Revelation chapter twelve. You can read the whole chapter to find out the actual verse.

Why then did God have to prepare hell for the devil and his angels? The answer is very simple: Jesus said, "Angels cannot die." Now, angels are real creatures, but they are creatures; they are a part of God's creation. They are higher in the order of creation than us. We are not the peak of God's creation, angels are. Evolutionists somehow have difficulty with that conception because where did the angels come from? Monkeys or wherever? You see problems therein. But we believe in angels. They are more intelligent than we are; they are stronger than we are; they are more flexible than we are; they are swifter in travel than we can be; they are superior to us in every way. In one particular they are significantly superior: we are mortal but angels are immortal.

I don't mean by that that they always existed. They had a beginning as we do, but they have no end. They cannot die whereas we can. That is why angels don't marry or reproduce; they are a fixed number. They cannot increase or decrease. They are there and God created them immortal. So since one third of them rebelled against God and are now evil angels, or demons as we call them, and they cannot die, what does God do with them? The answer is he prepares a place where they can be isolated from his universe. It is because they cannot die that he had to prepare the place to shut them up and shut them off from having influence.

Now, once we start there we ask, "Then if they are immortal and are in hell, this isolated place forever, what is their experience in that place?" The answer in the Bible is crystal clear: the devil and his angels will be tormented day and night forever and ever. There could not be a clearer and stronger statement in the Bible than that. They are immortal; they are confined to hell and they suffer torment. That word means "conscious pain". It can mean nothing else. Day and night, which means "without any let up", forever and ever. There is no stronger statement in the Greek language than forever and ever. It can only mean forever and ever. Literally translated, it says, "Until the ages of the ages." That is a very long time.

So, what do the annihilationists do with those statements about the devil and his angels being tormented forever and ever? The answer is they ignore them or they dismiss them, but they will not face them. There are, however, some who do say, "All right, let's accept that the angels suffer in hell forever, but human beings won't." But there is nothing in the Bible whatever to suggest that there is any difference of destiny between the devil and his angels and human beings who join them—none at all. In fact, we have clear statements that human beings will be tormented forever and ever.

For example, in that one verse where it says the devil will be tormented day and night forever and ever it says, "He will be tormented with the Beast and the False Prophet forever and ever." Those two at least are human beings. All antichrists are human beings and all false prophets are human beings. So here we have at least two human beings of whom it is said they will be tormented day and night forever and ever.

Then we have another much larger group mentioned: those people who in that final rule of that world dictator called the "Antichrist" who submit to having his number laser beamed onto their flesh so that they can buy and sell at the supermarket. That is an entirely credible scenario now since most of us are using numbers anyway on plastic, and they are already talking about tattooing or laser beaming numbers on your hand or your face so you can just go to the checkout and put your hand in a machine and everything will be debited to you.

It says in the book of Revelation that is how buying and selling will be done in the last days. It will take a great deal of courage to refuse to carry that number on your flesh because you will then not be able to buy and sell. You will be out of the market and unable to get enough food. It says of those who accept that number in order to buy food that they will be tormented forever and ever, the same phrase, "To the ages of the ages." When Jesus says to the goats, "Depart from me you cursed into the eternal punishment prepared for the devil and his angels," the plainest, simplest meaning of that language is, "Your destiny is the same as theirs." It is for that reason, though I hate to say it and wish I didn't have to say it, that I believe that the traditional understanding of hell as everlasting torment is what our New Testament teaches. That makes it horrible but I believe it to be the truth. I can't get around the plain statements of scripture.

Let me then go to another serious question, and probably the biggest shock that you will get in this chapter: who goes to hell? What do you have to do to "qualify"? There are two groups dealt with in scripture. One consists of carefree sinners, those who just do not listen to their conscience, who just do what they want to do. Altogether there are 120 sins listed in the New Testament that could take a person to hell. That is a frightening number. They are usually in separate lists of anywhere between half a dozen and ten in each list. There are two lists on the last two pages of the Bible. When you look at those lists and put them all together you have got 120 things that carefree sinners are doing that are on the broad road that leads to hell. As you would guess, sexual immorality figures frequently in those lists, whether fornication, sex before marriage, or adultery, sex after marriage with a partner other than your own. Those figure quite frequently. So does homosexual activity. How can we be silent when we know things could take a person into that kind of suffering that we have been talking about?

But it is a mistake if you think that sexual immorality is the main thing on those lists. There are plenty of other things on those lists. Idolatry occurs frequently. Now, we may say, "Well, that doesn't touch me, thank God. I've never bowed down to a lump of wood or stone and worshipped it." But when you find out that in those lists greed is classified as idolatry you have to think again. It is interesting that the commandment that most people have most difficulty with is the tenth, "Thou shalt not covet," which in simple language means, "Thou shalt not be greedy." Usually, it is our eyes that lead us into greed. The blind don't have that same problem. But greed is one of the things we are being taught through our commercial advertising and in many other ways. Greed, which is idolatry, is listed there.

Social injustices are also listed. Have you ever heard it said that the New Testament does not condemn slavery? Well, actually, it does. If you look up Paul's first letter to Timothy, in chapter one he lists the things that could take a person to hell. He mentions the murder of parents; well, that is pretty serious, isn't it? But straight away he mentions slave traders. By the way, if you thought that slavery had disappeared from our world you had better think again. It is still very much alive. But there are much more refined sins in that list of 120. Unbelief is classed as a sin that could take you to hell.

But one of the most surprising sins is in the second last list in Revelation 21. It says there that the cowardly go to the lake of fire. What does cowardly mean? It means those who for fear of people have not done or said what they knew to be right, those who have simply been cowards in standing up for what they know is right. How does that grab you? Of course, there are the more subtle sins of pride and other things. It is clear that there are many things that could take a person to hell.

There is also the surprise that things a person has not done, that unbelievers have not done, could take them there. Paul says that of those who do not know God, or those who do not obey the gospel. Now those are two different groups. Those who do not know God are those who have not heard the gospel but do know from their conscience and creation that there is a God to whom they are accountable. But those who do not obey the gospel are those who have heard it but have refused it. Only God knows who is in those two groups.

I am sure that if you are a Christian, so far you will have agreed with what I have said. Yes, such things put a person in danger of hell; they are on the broad way that leads to destruction. But now comes the shock. The Bible also talks about careless saints being in danger of hell. This is a real shock. You see, most of what we know about hell comes from the lips of Jesus. Within the four Gospels almost everything about hell is in the Gospel of Matthew. Now this is very significant. Why is there so little about hell in Luke, nothing about hell in Mark, and next to nothing about it in John? Why is it all in Matthew from cover to cover? Well, this is where we need the Bible study that looks at books as a whole. You see, there are four Gospels. Two of them were written for sinners and two for saints. Two were written for unbelievers and two for believers. Do you know which? John was not written for unbelievers; it is the most unsuitable to give an unbeliever. How they get past the first eighteen verses and still understand it I don't know. We are just hoping they will get as far as John 3:16 and that might "do the trick". But John is written for believers—mature believers. Matthew is written for believers but immature believers. It is only Mark and Luke that are written for sinners. They are the two Gospels you should use in evangelism.

Matthew is a manual of discipleship. Matthew doesn't just tell you what Jesus did; he collects Jesus' teaching and he puts all the teaching together in five major blocks, obviously to imply that Jesus is the new Moses. Moses gave us five books of the Law and now we have Jesus' five books on the kingdom, if you like. The theme is the kingdom in all five. In the first, which we call the "Sermon on the Mount", the theme is the lifestyle of the kingdom. Then we have the mission of the kingdom in the second—chapter ten. Then we have the growth of the kingdom in chapter thirteen. Then we have the community of the kingdom in chapter eighteen. Then we have the future of the kingdom in chapters twenty-four and twenty-five. All those five blocks of teaching are addressed not to sinners but to disciples.

It is a shock to realise that Jesus rarely, if ever, talked about hell to sinners. He gave a warning twice to Pharisees about hell, but every other warning he gave was given to born again disciples who had received him, believed in his name, and been born of God. That is the shock, because I am afraid that this unbiblical cliché, "Once saved always saved," is everywhere. But here we have the solemn thought that Jesus reserved most of his warnings about hell for his own followers, for those who were committed to him, for those who believed in him. Now do you appreciate the significance of that? I believe that one of the main reasons why preaching hell fell into disrepute was that it was preached by Christians who had no fear of it themselves. Do you understand what I am saying? It was a kind of, "You're going to hell; I'm not. I'm going to heaven." That kind of preaching is arrogant and offensive in the extreme. I believe no one is ready to preach on hell unless they fear that having preached to others, they may be thrown away themselves. It is believers who need to think about hell. It is the disciples of Christ who most need this message. I have explained that in full in my book *The Road to Hell*. That is why it will be such a shock, because this country is full of Christians who think, "I'm in no danger of finishing up there."

Therefore, we need to ask what kind of thing could lead a disciple of Jesus to hell? Here the surprise is that whereas with carefree sinners the emphasis is on what they do, and a little on what they don't do, with careless saints the emphasis is more on what they don't do. Now, if you study the Sermon on the Mount you will see that it is a teaching for Christians. It is not for sinners; it is not for unbelievers. It is almost impossible for believers, never mind for unbelievers. It is for those who are the sons of the kingdom.

It tells us that in the kingdom there is to be no anger, no lust, no worry. That is why you never see a Christian worried. You must have noticed. Now why do we laugh at that? Why do we treat that as a joke? Jesus said, "In my kingdom the sons don't worry because that's a libel on their Father in heaven." It is saying, "My Father cares more about his garden and his pets than he does about his kids. He feeds the birds of the air, he clothes the flowers of the field, but me, I'm just his child. I have to worry." That's libel. When you read the Sermon on the Mount that is a description of how Jesus expects his disciples to live. To say "Yes" when they mean "Yes" and "No" when they mean "No," not to get divorced and remarried, not to pay back evil for evil.

Yet there are at least five warnings in the Sermon on the Mount about hell. I have got a lot of books on my shelf expounding the Sermon on the Mount. Not one of them ever mentions that a disciple is ever in danger of hell. Yet Jesus says, "If you call someone a fool you are in danger of hellfire. If you look at a woman with lust you are heading there." When he finished this teaching for his disciples he said, "Now, there are two ways you can travel. There's a broad way that leads to destruction and there's a narrow way that leads to life," and he was speaking to his own followers. This is terribly important. Then when you get through to Matthew 25, which is entirely addressed to the twelve in the Sermon on the Mount, he talks about the virgins whose lamps ran out of oil, the man who buried his talent, and about those who did not visit him when he was in prison, or clothe him when he was naked. All things not done, do you notice that? All things neglected. That is all. Not bad things. Not crimes. Not vices. Just things not done that should have been done.

Now, I cannot get around this straight teaching. You see, what Jesus is saying is this: two things are needed to escape hell; one is forgiveness and the other is holiness. One of the clearest examples of this teaching is that in Luke's Gospel where Jesus tells a story of a feast to which people were invited but they made excuses. One said, "I've bought some oxen and I must try them out." Another said, "I've married a wife." Another said, "I've bought a field and I must go and inspect it," and they didn't come. So, the host of the feast was angry and said, "Go out into the highways and byways. Tell anybody to come. My house shall be full." It is a wonderful story to preach the gospel through. "Come and take your place. There's a place for you at the table."

It is in Luke's Gospel that you find that story for sinners. When you read the same story in Matthew there is a subtle twist. The story ends with everybody accepting the invitation, coming to the feast, but one man turns up without wedding clothes. He doesn't bother to change his clothes. The end of the story is that that man finishes in outer darkness and with weeping and gnashing of teeth. Matthew is addressed to believers. To unbelievers the message is, "Come, there's room for you at the feast." To believers the message is, "Come in the right clothes. Change your dirty clothes. Put on the righteousness that's available for you." Those who don't change their clothes are at the last turned away from the feast.

I remember reading *The Pilgrim's Progress* by John Bunyan and being greatly struck by a sentence right at the end, where Pilgrim arrives at the Jordan River, the black river of death, and his companion is scared of this river. He turns away and says, "I'm going to try and find another way across," and he walks down a side path. John Bunyan writes, "So I saw in my dream that there is a road to hell even from the gates of heaven." Now I believe, and I say this from my heart, that the church of today needs this message more than ever. Why should the Lord be sending such a message of repentance to Christians today? It is an extraordinary thing. It is a message that should be going to sinners. Why is it going to the church? I think because we have forgotten that we are in danger.

Let us take the clearest warning that Jesus ever gave. He said, "Don't fear those who can kill your body and afterwards do nothing else to you. Rather fear him who can ruin your body and soul in hell." Who was he talking to? Sinners? No. Pharisees? No. He was talking to the twelve apostles when he was sending them out to be missionaries. He didn't tell them to tell others about hell. He said, "Now you fear hell. As you go out to proclaim the kingdom, to raise the dead, cleanse the leper, cast out demons, heal the sick, and proclaim the kingdom has come, you fear hell." I believe one of the missing factors in much worship today is the fear of God. Have you noticed that? There is an awful lot of familiarity with God, not so much fear of God. I believe that one of the reasons is that believers no longer fear hell because the two are tied very closely together. Fear him who can destroy body and soul in hell. Now that is a sobering message, but I believe it is a much needed one.

Every writer of the New Testament has a warning about the danger of losing what you have found in Christ. I take those warnings desperately seriously. When Jesus said, "Abide in me. I am the true vine; you are the branches," he said, "Branches that do not abide in me, that do not stay in me, are cut out and are burned." I take that quite literally. Paul said, "You too will be cut off like the Jews, you too will be cut off, if you do not continue in God's kindness." This is not salvation by works; it is salvation by continued faith because forgiveness comes by faith and holiness comes by faith, but they both need to be appropriated. God is offering everything we need to be ready for heaven. But there are too many who have accepted the invitation to the feast who are not changing their clothes. That is the message I bring to you from Matthew's Gospel.

Now for some good news. There is no reason whatever why any of us should finish up in hell. Do you know why? First, we have the affection of the Father on our side. God loves us. He doesn't want anyone to finish up as useless rubbish in our universe. He has done everything he possibly could to save us from that. What more could he have done? He never prepared hell for us. He prepared hell for those angels, not us. God has no pleasure in throwing anybody away. He has pain when he has to do it. A picture of a vengeful God getting his own back on sinners by throwing them into the lake of fire, that is a libel on God. He has no pleasure in the death of the wicked, none at all. It must cause him immense grief that anyone made in his image should have to be thrown away.

We have the atonement of Jesus with us too. Do you know that Jesus descended into hell not after he died but before? He descended into hell for three hours, from noon until three o' clock. On that cross Jesus was in hell. How do I know? Well, very simple. There was total darkness, no natural light at all—couldn't see a thing. It was then that he cried out, "I thirst. I thirst." Above all, it was then that he cried out, *"Elohim, Elohim, lama sabachthani."* ("My God, my God, why have you forsaken me?"). That is hell. Jesus went through hell so that you need never go there. He did that to save you from it.

The third thing that is on your side is the assistance of the Holy Spirit. You say, "Well, I can never be holy. I can never be good enough for heaven." Yes, you can, because God gave you supernatural power. If there is one thing a Christian ought never to say it is, "I can't help it." There is a little word in Titus that says this: "He has given us the grace to say no," a very simple verse. Look, God loves you; Jesus died for you; the Spirit is available to you. Not only can you be forgiven, you can be made ready for heaven. It was Charles Wesley who wrote a famous hymn that has one verse in it, "A charge to keep I have, a God to glorify, a never-dying soul to save, and fit it for the sky." That last line is just as important as the other three. You see, we are called not to get people to make decisions; we are called to make disciples and to teach them how to live the way that Jesus taught. It is a long job. It can't be done in five minutes at the end of a meeting. It is a lifetime's job. But that is what Jesus is saying in Matthew's Gospel. You look up all his teaching on hell and you will find that almost every bit of it was not given to sinners but given to those who had left all, followed him, and who were committed to him.

Now, I hope that sobers you up. I know it has raised a lot of questions. Go and search the scriptures. Don't accept anything I say unless you can find it there. But look up every warning he gave and ask, "Who was he talking to at the time? Who was he warning?" But then also don't let yourself get into that panic, or that depression, that makes a person wake up every morning and say, "Am I saved or am I not?" You can have an assurance that you are on the way to heaven. But that assurance does not come from a decision that you made twenty years ago; it comes from a personal relationship you have now. It says, "The Spirit himself goes on witnessing with your spirit." You can be sure when you wake up in the morning that you are on the way. If you are walking with the Lord and with the Spirit you will have an assurance in your heart that you are heading for heaven. It is not a guarantee that you will arrive, it is an assurance that you are on the way.

One of the first things that happens to you when you sin is that you lose your assurance. When you get off the Way, when you get out of relationship. Stay in that relationship and you can walk in that daily assurance and be able to say, "I'm on my way." You see, salvation in scripture is a way. It is not an instantaneous thing. Anybody who repents has put a foot on the way, is walking on the way, and we are on the way to glory. The Spirit wants to give us that assurance of God's love that he wants us to make it, that he is on our side. There is nothing else that can separate you from his love—nothing, only you. But if you continue in his love, as Paul says, you will not be cut off. That fact that two and a half million left Egypt and only two arrived in Canaan is used by three different writers of the New Testament as a warning for believers. He does not want to save us *from* only; he wants to save us *to*. He wants to get us to heaven and he wants to get us ready for heaven so that when we arrive it is the saints who go marching in.

That is probably the most serious thing and probably a surprise to you. Perhaps you didn't expect to hear that. You thought I was going to tell you that all those sinners out there are heading to hell and they are in great danger. They are and it is a motivation to us to go and rescue them while we can. But having said that, keep the fear of it in your own heart lest having preached to them you be cast away yourself.

So, hell is a serious topic and it has a profound effect on Christians. It affects our worship. I believe it will affect our worship in two ways. First, it will bring us to a profounder gratitude to God for what he has done for us. When you take bread and wine at Communion, you will be so grateful. You will want to say, "Thank you, thank you, thank you." In Greek, you would say, *"Eucharisteo, eucharisteo, eucharisteo."* That is what "Eucharist" means; it means — it is a thank you that he would go through hell so that I need not go there. It will produce a gratitude but it will also produce a reverence, and a fear of God will be restored to the church. That will not just show in worship, it will show in holiness too. Because when you are not afraid that sin will cause you to lose what you have got you won't take it so seriously.

It would be totally unfair of God to send an unbeliever to hell for adultery but to shut his eyes when a believer persists in it, wouldn't it? Yet many are saying, "I'm all right." They are saying, "Well, she may be a prostitute, she may be on drugs, but praise the Lord, when she was nine years old, she made the great decision." That kind of talk is crazy talk. The New Testament says, "Follow after holiness without which no man will see the Lord." It will have an effect on our evangelism. We are not just trying to bring people a little happiness; we are not just trying to give them a solution to their daily problems. We are rescuing them from hell. That is what evangelism is: rescuing people from a useless, godless eternity. That is what we are after. We are not just trying to do them a good turn, or add a little nice dimension to their life. "You should come to church. We're very warm there, it's very friendly, you'd enjoy it." That is not what we are after. We are not after getting people into a religious club. We are snatching people from the fire. That has always been a major motivation in missionary work. It will affect us in so many ways.

Finally, those who fear hell find it much easier to face martyrdom. When Jesus said, "Don't fear those who can kill your body but rather fear him who can destroy body and soul in hell," he was saying that the cure for fear of man is fear of God. The cure for little fears is the big fear. That is true. You lose your little fears when you have got a big fear. The big fear is the fear of finishing up there. When you are more afraid of that than anything else, you can face anything or anyone. Those who fear God fear no one and nothing else. I think of one of the early martyrs, Polycarp of Smyrna. They threatened to burn him alive on a red-hot sheet of iron. Polycarp said, "You threaten me with the fire that kills the body; I fear the fire that destroys me forever." He went to his death.

It puts courage into Christians. If you fear God it cures your other fears. You don't need therapy for all the other ones then. You can fear the Lord. There is as much about the fear of God in the New Testament as in the Old. It is empowered Christian living. For our God is a consuming fire. Therefore, let us approach him with reverence and awe as we worship him.

That is enough about hell; I want to get you to heaven. So, in the next chapter we are going to go for glory. Amen.

Chapter 6

The Reward of Heaven

The existence of hell has been attacked for many reasons, even among believers, but nobody argues about heaven. Isn't it interesting? We usually argue about the things we don't like, and the things we do like we don't want to argue about. Yet unbelievers do argue about heaven and they do criticise us for believing in it. There are two criticisms in particular. Some unbelievers accuse us of a harmless delusion. They say it is a product of human imagination, compensation for a difficult life here. It is like a child's fairy tale with its pearly gate and golden streets—quite incredible, and so, just as there are jokes about hell, there are also jokes about heaven, usually including the Apostle Peter.

Even some of the Jews used to make jokes about it; the Sadducees didn't believe in heaven and that is why they were sad, you see! Now you will remember that! They came to Jesus once and said, "A woman's husband died, then his brother married her, and she had seven husbands altogether. Now what a mess it's going to be in heaven. In the resurrection, whose wife will she be?" They sneered to each other, and Jesus said, "You don't know the scripture, and you don't know the power of God." He said, "In heaven, you are neither married" [that's for men], "nor given in marriage," [that's the women], "but you will be like the angels who cannot die." That is, by the way, where he said, "Angels cannot die."

Others have accused us of being guilty of a dangerous distraction, not just a harmless delusion. They say this is escapism from real life; this makes people content with bad conditions here, and often spirituals are cited. Do you remember the song the slaves used to sing, "I got shoes; you got shoes; when I get to heaven, I'm gonna put on my shoes, gonna walk all over God's heaven"? Reformers said, "This is keeping the slaves happy without shoes, by teaching them about heaven." It was, in fact, Charles Kingsley, the author of *Tom and the Water Babies*, who called such hopes of heaven, even though he was an Anglican clergyman, "the opiate" of the people". Karl Marx picked that phrase up and changed it to "the opium of the people", but he said that Christianity is opium; it's a drug just to keep people happy in the bad social conditions here and now.

The world criticised the church for talking too much about heaven. I am afraid the result was that the church listened to the world and allowed the world to set its agenda. Now we have very little about heaven in the church at all. Have you noticed that hardly any choruses are being written about heaven, never mind any hymns about hell, such as we used to sing? So we have fallen in with the world's criticism and there has been a swing from too much thought about the future, to far too little. We will have to get back on course and get a balance with the Word of God.

So, I want to address the subject of heaven. Now the word "heaven" in scripture is a very flexible word. It is used, for example, of the air through which the birds fly; the birds flying in heaven. Going up a little further, it is used of the place where the clouds are; it is used for beyond that, the blue sky. In fact, the Hebrews thought of heaven almost in layers, and they talked about the third heaven and the seventh heaven. In fact, Paul once said that he knew a man (presumably himself) who had an experience of being disembodied, a possible out-of-body experience in which his spirit went and visited the third heaven. He saw things that were so marvellous that God had to keep a thorn in his flesh to keep him humble afterwards. So, heaven means an awful lot of things in scripture, but highest heaven is God's address. When you talk to God, you talk to God in heaven.

A key to understanding heaven in the Bible is to study the relationship between heaven and earth, not so much in spatial terms, but in spiritual terms. You find this, that at the beginning of the Bible before sin had got into our world, heaven and earth were very close– so close that God could take a stroll down here, and Adam heard the sound of the Lord God walking in the garden in the cool of the evening. But as soon as you read about sin coming in, you get a sense that heaven withdrew, that a great gulf opened up between earth and heaven so that God in heaven is a long way away. In fact, if you want him to hear you will have to call on the name of the Lord. You will have to worship with a loud shout, so that he can hear. Do you get that impression as you go through the Old Testament?

Typical of this is Jacob's dream at Bethel where he saw this huge staircase or ladder stretching all the way from earth right up to heaven. He saw angels ascending and descending. That again is a clue. Why are there so many more angels in the Old Testament than the New? It is not just because it covers a greater period of time. There is a profound reason. God is way up there in highest heaven. We are way down here on earth. How do we communicate with each other? The answer is through angels. They are God's messengers who come down with messages for us and who ascend with messages for him. So, you have this tremendous sense of a gulf between heaven and earth all the way through the Old Testament—a long distance to highest heaven where God lives.

But as soon as Jesus comes to earth the gap closes; it is very striking. I want to look at one of the interesting things that Jesus said in John chapter three—incidentally, everybody knows verse sixteen, but few know verse fourteen or verse twelve, and they are just as important. Here is one of those verses. Jesus said, "No man has been up into heaven, but the Son of Man who has come down from heaven who is in heaven." Did you notice that last phrase? In other words, when Jesus came, he did not leave heaven, he brought it with him. Heaven was now back in touch with earth. The kingdom of heaven was at hand, and to be "at hand" is to be within your reach. You can just reach out and grab it, so the kingdom of heaven is here now. Heaven was touching earth again when Jesus came. The gap is being closed again. Heaven is very real and very near, and Jesus was still living in heaven even while he was on earth. "No man has ascended into heaven except the Son of Man who came down from heaven, who is in heaven."

Then the other verse in John 3 is this: Jesus says, "If I've told you earthly things and you don't believe me, how will you believe if I talk to you about heavenly things?" If people don't believe what Jesus says about this life, how on earth will they believe what he says about the next? He is the only reliable source of information we have about the other world because he is the only one who has been there and come back to tell us.

Now let us talk about heaven. At the end of the Bible, we have a new heaven and a new earth. This is rather important because, you see, most people think of going to heaven as going somewhere else, but God has a future for this earth. There is going to be a new earth. I wonder when you last heard a preacher talk about the new earth for you. I love talking about it. I was in Sydney, Australia, about five miles from Bondi Beach, and I said, "In the new earth, there will be no sun, no sea, and no sex." Their faces dropped. They looked as if they wanted to leave the meeting immediately and get back down to Bondi Beach to enjoy all three while they could. I'll tell you something else. Though none of those three things will be there in the new earth, you won't even miss them. It will be so wonderful, but it will be different.

But you see, God doesn't want just to redeem men and women, he wants to redeem all creation. He wants to make all things new and not just all people, because this poor old planet has been so exploited and polluted. You know, the humanist thinks this is the only Planet Earth that humankind will ever have to live on. That is why they are panicking. That is why the green movement is in danger of becoming a religion, propitiating Mother Earth and going all the way back to the fertility cults of Baal, you mark my words. Now Christians are concerned about the environment, but we are not panicking, because we know that the same God who made this one is going to make a new earth. There will be a new city; a big one.

Now, I do a bit of architecture in my spare time, mostly designing church buildings to look not like church buildings, but to be a home for God's people. I am interested in architecture. One of the problems architects have is this: how to plan a large building or city and yet keep the scale human. I have studied many "new" cities—Brasilia in Brazil, and Canberra. It is interesting that in both cases, they dammed up a stream to create water through the middle of the city. That is in imitation of the New Jerusalem, but in none of those once-new cities have I seen this human scale.

I can't wait to see the architecture of the New Jerusalem. How can God build a city that big and yet keep it like a village; keep it human; keep it to size. Do you realise what the size of that city will be, the city whose builder and maker is God, and the city which Abraham was looking for? It would just fit inside the moon if the moon were hollow. It would cover about two-thirds of the continent of Europe. It is about fifteen hundred miles each way, three ways, so it is either going to be a pyramid or a cube, but I don't know how God will plan that, I just cannot wait to see it. It will be the most perfect city. As soon as you see it, you will say, "Oh, I wish I could live there forever." God will say, "There's a room marked for you."

Now I want to prove to you that the Bible is inspired by God and could only have been written by God using human authors. I learnt something in one of the most interesting books that I have. I don't know if you know what polarised light is. Normal light bounces at us from all kinds of directions. It is reflected at us, so normal light, the lines of light are going all ways. Polarised light goes in straight lines. If you have got sunglasses with polarised lenses, it only lets straight light through and all that bounced light is cut off. Now, if you get two polarised sunglasses and turn them at right angles, you get crossed-polarised light, a very pure light.

Now let us take all the precious stones some ladies wear in their rings and in their ears. I have got a bit of a shock for you. If you take a very thin slice of a precious stone, a jewel, and look at it through cross-polarised light, two sunglass lenses at right angles, one of two things will happen. Either that stone will go all the colours of the rainbow, but in its own unique pattern, or it will go black and have no colour at all. Now, wouldn't you like to know which is which? Some ladies will be very cross with their husbands afterwards! For example, diamonds go black in pure light, rubies go black in pure light. Garnets go black in pure light, but other stones go all the colours of the rainbow. Now, I have got a book by a scientist with many of the stones that go all the colours of the rainbow, but different patterns. However, in the New Jerusalem, the only precious stones that God uses are the stones that go all the colours of the rainbow in pure light and none of the others is used. There is no way that the Apostle John could have known that when he wrote the book of Revelation, because it was only a few decades ago that we found polarised light and have been able to discover this. How then could John the Apostle possibly have known? Can you imagine what the New Jerusalem will look like?

There is another point of interest—the *shape* of the stones. The crystal shape of precious stones is different. All the stones that are used in the New Jerusalem are angular and easily fitted together in a building, whereas the crystalline form of many other stones is more like a round marble and very difficult to build with. God has used none of those in the New Jerusalem. How could John possibly have known this? Only God knew it, and again I mention this to stress that we are not talking about fairy tales now. We are talking about something quite real. To me that is just proof that the Bible is inspired by God's Holy Spirit because nobody but God until modern times could have known that.

What will life be like in that city? There will be fruit trees with a new crop every month. Fruit is obviously going to be a major part of the diet. There is one tree that reappears in that city that has been absent from all the pages of the Bible since the beginning. That is the tree of life, the tree that will give you all the minerals, all the carbohydrates, all the proteins and all the vitamins that you need to go on living, because there is no reason why our bodies should wear out. They are most efficient machines and they can reproduce themselves. You change your skin every six weeks. Most of the dust in your bedroom is your skin. In theory, your body should be able to go on renewing itself, but in practice it starts winding down and no scientist knows why. The only reason why my body dies and rots is because it belonged to a rotten sinner. God would not let my body see corruption if I had been holy all my life.

Well, what will life be like there? I want to give you fourteen points — seven negative and seven positive. Seven is the perfect number, so that is good for heaven. First of all, what will life not be like in heaven, in the New Jerusalem, in this metropolis? By the way, the gates will always be open so you will be able to explore the whole universe freely. You will be able to step into space as freely as Jesus ascended and be able to take your holiday on Mars, go anywhere. What a wonderful universe it will be to explore!

On the negative side, what will not be there? Well, I have said already, there will be no sex. Now it is important to realise that marriage is for life. It does not survive the grave. It is "Till death us do part." If you meet again, you will meet again as brother and sister, not as husband and wife. It is quite wrong to encourage people to think their marriage will be renewed beyond the grave. The Mormons teach that. You can be married for eternity if you get married in one of their temples, but I believe Jesus was right when he said, "You are neither married nor given in marriage." That is why, if death intervenes in a marriage, the partner is perfectly free to marry someone else. Indeed, it could be a tribute to their first marriage if they do. Some people have an inhibition on that score. They needn't. No sex; therefore, blood relationships are ended as far as human blood is concerned. You will belong to another family there.

Secondly, no suffering will be there — no hospitals, no sanatoria, no cemeteries, no pain, no handicaps, no deformities. There may be scars, which will be badges of honour. I believe Jesus will have his nail prints and Paul will have a more scarred body than anyone else probably, but they are scars he bore with pride and honour. He had suffered for Jesus, but handicaps, no; pain, no; suffering, no; separation, no.

Isn't life full of goodbyes? I spend a lot of time in airport lounges and I love watching people. You know, sometimes they rush towards each other with arms outstretched and seem to blend into one; other times you see them sorrowfully pulling themselves away reluctantly. You just see so many goodbyes. There will be no goodbyes in heaven.

That is probably why there is no more sea, because sea separates people. You go overseas, and sea to the Jew was always a barrier that cut them off from others. There will be no such thing, no distance. No sorrow; I think one of the loveliest little phrases in the Bible—it is repeated twice at the end of the Bible—is the one which says, "God will wipe away all tears from their eyes." Have you ever heard a parent say, "Don't cry; no need to cry any more, it's all over." God will wipe away every tear; no sorrow. No shadows; no darkness; no night—just pure light everywhere; twenty-four hours; there will be no street lamps in the New Jerusalem, just pure light. No sanctuaries; no temples; no cathedrals; no churches—hallelujah for that! They are a liability, aren't they? It costs many millions each year to repair cathedrals, but you won't see any spires in the New Jerusalem because God will be there. There will be no need for any reminders pointing to heaven.

There will be no sin, no pride, no greed, no lust, no lies; nothing to defile or spoil it, and, therefore, no temptations. Can you imagine that? It is all yours. You can enjoy everything. There is nothing forbidden. The tree of knowledge of good and evil does not pop up again, just the tree of life. No temptations. What a relief that will be! No more curse; only blessing; that is the negative side; that is pretty good, but now listen to the positive side.

First of all, there will be rest. Now that is not sitting in an armchair doing nothing. People think of heaven as a lot of armchairs with RIP embroidered on them. It is not that kind of rest, because, actually, that is not the rest that you would like. You would not enjoy doing nothing. Rest is doing something you enjoy doing, that is stimulating, that leaves you more refreshed after you have done it. That is the kind of rest there will be. Working day and night, it says; serving him day and night, twenty-four hour shifts every day, and yet never getting tired. I can't imagine it, can you?

It will be a place of reward. Some people think that rewards are immoral, that you shouldn't have to need the incentive of a reward. Well, I don't believe it, because Jesus offered reward. He said, "Great is your reward in heaven." Mind you, it is sobering. When I used to go behind the Iron Curtain or when I went behind the Bamboo Curtain, I thought, "How much greater reward these people will get than we in the West. We just play games. We play church, but to them, what a reward!" There will be great differences in heaven. It won't be one gigantic egalitarian socialist republic in which everybody gets the same. Some people will get a great reward, some a little reward.

That brings me to the third thing—responsibility. There will be jobs; not preachers, not evangelists, not missionaries, but people to look after God's universe; people to be creative in art and music. "The treasures of the nations will be brought into it," it says, and what riches there are. If you go to Israel today, you have got nearly eighty-five nations who have come back to one country and they have each brought their own music, and their own dance, and their own art. What a rich variety of cultures that has made. There is a whole new music that has emerged from that. Think what it will be like when all the cultures of the world and people of every kindred and tribe and tongue are brought into that city, and bring with them their culture and their insights and the riches of their background.

It will be a place of revelation. You will know all that you want to know. You will finally be able to settle the matter of predestination and freewill. You will actually be able to go and ask Paul about all those parts of his Epistles that are difficult to understand. Can you imagine it? You won't have to go up to someone and say, "Could I just have two minutes with you?" You could say, "Do you mind if I just have the next thousand years to discuss these issues?" A place of revelation; a place where you will know even as you have been known; where you will know God as well as he knows you now, and he knows how many hairs there are on your head. If you are dark-haired you probably have about a hundred and twenty thousand. If you are fair-haired you probably have about a hundred and five; if you are ginger you probably have about ninety-five thousand, but God knows the exact number. Of course, it is an easier task for him as you get older, but that is how well he knows you. It says that we shall know, no longer looking through a dark mirror, but looking face to face. All your questions answered—think of it. We have a lot of questions to be answered. There are mysteries; there are things we do not understand, and it is wise for a Christian to admit they don't know when they are asked about something they are unsure about. It is wiser to say, "I don't know, but I know him and I believe he knows, and one day I will," rather than try to explain all the mystery. We are not God, but we will know the answers one day.

A place of righteousness, of positive goodness, of love and joy and peace and patience and kindness and generosity and faithfulness and meekness and self-control; fancy living in a world where there is nothing but goodness. Again, it is almost beyond our imagination. It will be a place of rejoicing. Every picture of heaven is a happy picture—a picture of a party, a picture of a feast, a banquet, a celebration. One of the most amazing things I ever read from Jesus' lips was this. Jesus said, "Faithful servants of mine, I will sit them at table and I will wait on them." Can you imagine sitting at a table and seeing a plate of food put in front of you and you look up and it is Jesus who brought it for you? I'm afraid I'll feel like Peter who didn't want his feet washed, but that is what he says. I tell you, if a person reading this book repents of their sin today, they are going to have a party up there. They have a celebration when one sinner repents. What will it be like when the saints come marching in?

It will be a place of recognition. People say, "How will I recognise anybody?" The answer is: immediately you will know. How did Peter, James and John know Jesus was talking to Moses and Elijah? They had been dead for centuries. They just knew. That is how it will be with you. "Why, there's Noah over there, I always wondered what he looked like. There's Paul, and that's dear old Peter." Well, let us move on. We still haven't touched on the best.

What turns a house into a home? Fitted carpets, kitchen gadgets? No. What turns a house into a home is the people who are there. Home is where your loved ones are. The real question we need to ask about heaven is: who will be there? I shall just finish with four answers. First, the saints will be there. Now, many of them we will have heard of—the great saints—and we will be able to talk to them, get to know them, but there will be millions we have never heard of. We will have all eternity to get to know them. Isn't that exciting? The saints will be there; so many unnamed, plenty of those who have been named, but plenty of unnamed ordinary people who were saints of God and who overcame. All your spiritual relatives will be there. Your physical relatives may not be, but your spiritual relatives will be; one huge family.

Isn't it true that when you are converted you feel closer to your spiritual relatives than your physical relatives? Of course, you have a responsibility to remain in total communication with your physical relatives. You may be the only link they have with the Lord, but deep down you can't share with them like you can share with your fellow believers. You can meet a stranger and find out he is a Christian and you can be talking within five minutes as if you have known each other for twenty years. Have you noticed that? People are surprised. "How long have you known that guy?" "Well, I just met him." "But you're talking as if you've known him twenty years!" "Well, in a sense I have, because we've had everything in common for twenty years. We've known the same Lord for twenty years." The saints will be there.

The angels will be there, and you may well recognise some of them. They do not appear with a harp and a long white nightie and wings. I mean, if that were how they appeared, you could not possibly entertain an angel unawares. The Bible says, "Be given to hospitality, for thereby some have entertained angels unawares." Listen, they appear like humans. You could have given a hitchhiker a lift and had an angel in your car. You may discover it when you get there.

A young lady once told me that she was walking alone through the dark streets of one of our cities on her way back home. A young man leapt out from the shadows, grabbed her, and was tearing her clothes off and was obviously going to rape her. She cried out to the Lord of Hosts, and another young man came round the corner, pushed that young man off her, took her arm and said, "Come on, Helen. I'll see you home." She got to her home, put the key in the door, turned around to thank him, but he wasn't there and there was no one in the street. She will recognise him when she meets him again in glory. We don't need to be aware of the angels. We need to have the faith that God surrounds us with his hosts. We will recognise them and we'll say, "Why, I gave you a lift in my car. I thought you were just a guy from down the road." Always be aware that there are angelic beings around us. So, the angels will be there.

Jesus will be there—the Lamb with horns and the Lion. He says, "I will come and get you so that where I am, you may be too." That is heaven. I don't know whether I'll look at his face first or his hands—I'll probably look from one to the other. However will we thank him? He will probably say to us, "I didn't do this for me. I did it for my Father. I got all the kingdoms of this world back in my hands so that I could give them back to him and he can be all in all," which brings me to the climax.

God will be there. You will see him as King. You will see his throne; you will worship him, and yet you will be able to call him "Abba", "Dad", "Father". Here is the most amazing thing I discovered in my Bible. I find many Christians have never spotted it. The Bible does not talk about us going to heaven to live forever with the Father. It talks about just the opposite. It says, "The Father is moving to earth to live with us forever." Isn't that amazing? You see, the New Jerusalem comes down out of heaven to earth, but it is not just the New Jerusalem that comes down, it is God who comes down, and the angels are amazed. They say, "Look! Behold, the dwelling place of God is with men!" Not the dwelling place of men is now with God, but the dwelling place of God is now with men.

Here is the most amazing truth. God is going to change his address at the very end of history. He is moving in with us. Well, the angels have been down here and his Son has been down here, but the great climax of the Bible is that God moves house. His dwelling place will be with us in that new earth. This will be the centre of the new universe. Isn't that remarkable? God, from highest heaven, moves down here. We will no longer say, "Our Father in heaven." We will be able to say, "Our Father, with us on earth." That is the climax in my Bible. God loves us so much that he wants to live with us and move in with us. He wants to be our God so that we might be his people, and the dwelling place of God at the end of the Bible is with people—Emmanuel, God with us.

Well, that is enough about heaven. If we spent more time on it, we would get so impatient with earth that we would not be any use down here. God has told us enough about heaven to make us sure that it exists, that it is being prepared. It is not just heaven; it is a new heaven and a new earth. It is right here that the New Jerusalem, built out in space, will come to be the capital city of God's kingdom. At the end of the Bible, the kingdom of heaven is established on earth; as we pray every day, "Your kingdom come on earth, as it is in heaven." Amen.

BOOKS BY DAVID PAWSON
AVAILABLE FROM DAVIDPAWSON.COM

BIBLE COMMENTARIES

UNLOCKING THE BIBLE Omnibus ISBN 978 0 007166 66 4
UNLOCKING THE BIBLE - Charts, diagrams and images ISBN 978 1 911173 17 5

Introducing GENESIS ISBN 978 1 911173 80 9
Introducing The OLD TESTAMENT and HEBREW POETRY ISBN 978 1 911173 90 8

A Commentary on GENESIS Chapters 1-25 ISBN 978 1 911173 82 3
A Commentary on EXODUS ISBN 978 1 911173 85 4
A Commentary on Selected PSALMS ISBN 978 1 911173 91 5
A Commentary on ECCLESIASTES ISBN 978 1 911173 98 4
A Commentary on ISAIAH ISBN 978 1 913472 05 4
A Commentary on JEREMIAH ISBN 978 1 911173 76 2
A commentary on DANIEL ISBN 978 1 911173 06 9
A Commentary on THE MINOR PROPHETS ISBN 978 1 911173 94 6
A Commentary on ZECHARIAH ISBN 978 1 911173 38 0

A Commentary on the Gospel of MATTHEW ISBN 978 1 913472 09 2
A Commentary on the Gospel of MARK ISBN 978 1 909886 26 1
A Commentary on the Gospel of LUKE ISBN 978 1 911173 21 2
A Commentary on the Gospel of JOHN ISBN 978 1 909886 27 8
A Commentary on ACTS ISBN 978 1 909886 38 4
A Commentary on ROMANS ISBN 978 1 909886 78 0
A Commentary on 1 & 2 CORINTHIANS ISBN 978 1 909886 95 7
A Commentary on GALATIANS ISBN 978 1 909886 29 2
A Commentary on EPHESIANS ISBN 978 1 909886 98 8
A Commentary on PHILIPPIANS ISBN 978 1 909886 74 2
A Commentary on COLOSSIANS ISBN 978 1 913472 17 7
A Commentary on 1 & 2 THESSALONIANS ISBN 978 1 909886 73 5
A Commentary on 1 & 2 TIMOTHY, TITUS, PHILEMON - The Personal Letters ISBN 978 1 909886 70 4
A Commentary on HEBREWS ISBN 978 1 909886 33 9
A Commentary on JAMES ISBN 978 1 909886 72 8
A commentary on 1 & 2 PETER ISBN 978 1 909886 79 7
A Commentary on the LETTERS OF JOHN ISBN 978 1 909886 69 8
A Commentary on JUDE ISBN 978 1 909886 28 5
A Commentary on the book of REVELATION ISBN 978 1 909886 25 4

EXPLAINING SERIES
A CHRISTIAN DISCIPLESHIP TRAINING PROGRAMME

TOPICAL BOOKS

CPSIA information can be obtained
at www.ICGtesting.com
Printed in the USA
BVHW041330240721
612646BV00028B/956